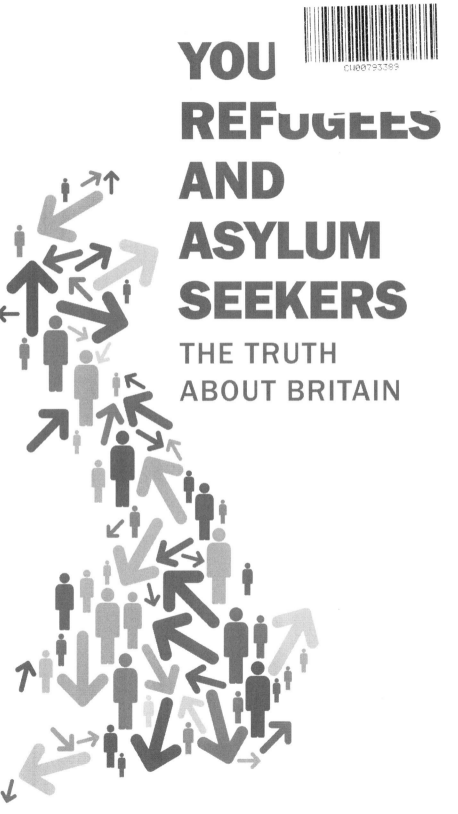

# YOU REFUGEES AND ASYLUM SEEKERS

## THE TRUTH ABOUT BRITAIN

**Other books you may be interested in:**

*Active Social Work with Children with Disabilities*
By Julie Adams and Diana Leshone          ISBN 978-1-910391-94-5

*Observing Children and Families: Beyond the Surface*
By Gill Butler          ISBN 978-1-910391-62-4

*Psychosocial and Relationship-based Practice*
By Claudia Megele          ISBN 978-1-909682-97-9

*The Critical Years: Child Development from Conception to Five*
By Tim Gully          ISBN 978-1-909330-73-3

*The W Word: Witchcraft Labelling and Child Safeguarding in Social Work Practice*
By Prospera Tedam and Awura Adjoa          ISBN 978-1-912096-00-8

Titles are also available in a range of electronic formats. To order please go to our website www.criticalpublishing.com or contact our distributor NBN International, telephone 01752 202301 or email orders@nbninternational.com

# YOUNG REFUGEES AND ASYLUM SEEKERS

## THE TRUTH ABOUT BRITAIN

DECLAN HENRY

First published in 2020 by Critical Publishing Ltd

British Library Cataloguing in Publication Data
A CIP record for this book is available from the British Library

ISBN: 978-1-913063-97-9

This book is also available in the following e-book formats:
MOBI ISBN: 978-1-913063-98-6
EPUB ISBN: 978-1-913063-99-3
Adobe e-book ISBN: 978-1-913453-00-8

Cover design by Out of House Ltd
Text design by Greensplash Limited
Project Management by Newgen Publishing UK
Printed and bound in Great Britain by 4edge, Essex

Critical Publishing
3 Connaught Road
St Albans
AL3 5RX

www.criticalpublishing.com

Paper from responsible sources

The names of any child or young person featured in this book have been changed. In some cases, other details have also been changed in order to protect identities and to ensure anonymity.

The author has used the words Britain and the UK (United Kingdom) interchangeably in the text. While young refugees and asylum seekers are located in all parts of the UK, the largest number are in Britain. The UK's government (including the Home Office) is based in Britain and it is here that legislation affecting the lives of these young people is determined.

*Dedicated to my friend, Joanne.*

# Contents

# Meet the author

Declan Henry is a creative non-fiction writer and comes from a distinguished academic background. He studied at two of London's elite universities – Goldsmiths College and King's College. He holds a Bachelor of Arts (Honours) degree in Education and Community Studies and a Master of Science degree in Mental Health Social Work. Declan is a registered social worker and is the author of seven other books and numerous published articles. He has written on a wide range of diverse topics, including mental health, transgender people, Islam and young offenders. He is the bronze winner of the 2017 Independent Publisher Book Award in the LGBT non-fiction list for his book *Trans Voices – Becoming Who You Are*. He is also a reviewer for the *New York Journal of Books*. Declan was born in County Sligo in the Irish Republic and now lives in Kent. www.declanhenry.co.uk

# Foreword

*Lord Alfred Dubs*

The world is facing the greatest refugee crisis since the Second World War. With no prospect of an end to global conflicts or persecution, the crisis is set to continue. And with the growing threat of climate change to the world's poorest communities, the refugee crisis and global migration will only increase as drought, crop failure and flooding drive even more people from their homes.

The global refugee population is 30 million with an additional 35 million internally displaced people. Swept up in this refugee crisis are thousands, perhaps millions, of children. Many of them fall victim to smugglers, or worse, they are trafficked, which means they have 'earnt' their way to Europe through slavery, prostitution or enforced labour. Thousands of children simply disappear en route, absorbed by criminals and their networks. As we all know, having seen the pitiful photo of Alan Kurdi's body washed up on a beach, their journeys to safety are perilous and can end in tragedy.

Some finally reach refugee camps. But anyone who has visited the refugee camps in Greece or Calais cannot fail to be moved by the plight of the refugee children stranded there. There can be few sights more moving and distressing than children with no family, in a foreign country where they don't speak the language, living in makeshift shelters, overcrowded camps or rough on the streets.

No two refugee stories are the same, but, especially for child refugees, there are common themes, trauma being the most common shared experience. Violence and despair have catapulted them from their homes; they have then endured terrible and frightening journeys only to find themselves in dangerous camps where violence and exploitation are commonplace. Each trauma compounds the last.

For those refugee children fortunate enough to eventually find a home in a safe country, hopefully in a loving environment, their journeys do not end there. The business of rebuilding their lives is slow and underscored by the trauma of leaving their home, of their journey and of their time in the camps. Many will need specialist help.

Having fled their homes and after travelling often for months or even years, another common theme is the impact of missing years of schooling. Once safe, refugee children, like all children, need the hope, opportunity and means to succeed that only education can provide.

This is not to say that refugee children cannot thrive. The same resilience and determination that means they were able to cross continents to safety is a powerful force. This resilience, when combined with the right support, and access to education and opportunities, stands these children in good stead.

While achieving greatness is not a measure by which I would want our society to judge a human being's value, refugee children can and do go on to achieve great things. Others simply heal and live their lives peacefully and in safety.

Being a refugee doesn't have to cost a child their future. Dedicated and professional social workers across the country play a vital role in making sure these children get the support they need to live fulfilled lives.

I believe that the way we treat the most vulnerable people is a test of who we are, what kind of country we hope to live in and what humanity we have. Britain has a proud tradition of humanity and hospitality towards child refugees. In 1938 the UK government welcomed 10,000 refugee children from Germany, Austria and Czechoslovakia, including me. I would like us to, once again, respond to a global refugee crisis with the same humanity and kindness we showed then by committing to taking 10,000 child refugees from Europe and the region over the next ten years.

I hope as a society our leaders will have the courage to talk more honestly about migration and the enormous benefits it brings to recipient countries. The coronavirus crisis has underlined, for instance, the extent to which our National Health Service depends on migrants. I also hope the vital work of social workers, who are on the front line of helping refugee children deal with trauma, assimilate into their new societies and reach their potential, is fully appreciated. Social workers are often invisible but the impact they can have on young lives can be transformative.

# Personal endorsement

*Philip Ishola*, Independent Policy Adviser in Trafficking, Child Protection, Human Rights

First, thank you Declan Henry, for the opportunity to read such an insightful, powerful and challenging book.

When I met Declan to talk about some of the issues that impact on the lives of some of the most vulnerable in our society (children and young people arriving in the UK from abroad unaccompanied by their parents or caregivers), I was immediately struck by Declan's ability to understand how our system fails them. He recognises the challenges presented to the many excellent professionals working within a broken system and breaks down the core values that drive our professionals to care and support children.

Upon reading *Young Refugees and Asylum Seekers: The Truth about Britain*, I was struck by how this book contextualises the obvious issues we know to be true and provides a clear unwavering narrative to challenge, encourage, empower and support the change needed to allow the professional and empathic nature of caring for such children to shine through.

So, when asked to write the foreword I did so with pleasure. It filled me with sadness, however, to think of the plight of some children and young people, but also inspired me to learn that there are many people like Declan who work to ensure children are seen as children first.

While reading, I noted Declan's thoughts about the world of *'secrets and lies'* in which professionals sometimes feel they operate when working with these children and young people, and how for children and young people *'secrets and lies are part of the young person's sense of survival'*. A great observation and it got me thinking.

In my professional work I know when it comes to these children and young people there is a struggle, a professional struggle, between what is right and what is expected by child safeguarding guidance that is corrupted by a toxic narrative which normalises something we know to be wrong, *'secrets and lies'*. A narrative that separates some children and young people from others and creates a two-tier system where they arrive in the UK from abroad, unaccompanied by their parents or caregivers, and are seen, on the one hand, as children in need and, on the other, as some kind of 'issue' that has to be dealt with.

This book explores why this happens and how the toxic narrative and polar opposite agenda of immigration and border protection drives the child safeguarding and protection responses. This puts social work practitioners in extremely difficult professional quandaries: to do what their empathic instincts, training and children's legislation compel them to do (care, support and where required protect), or adhere to the 'opposite' requirements that influence all aspects of work with these children and young people.

It is as if we operate in the world of 'Alice' where two brains are required – one needed to do everything in our power to meet their needs and the other to enable us to do what is not in their best interests. This 'Alice in Wonderland' world is not only damaging to the professional but also to the child and young person and I would go as far as to say damaging to the very soul of the child social care philosophy and practice.

*Young Refugees and Asylum Seekers: The Truth about Britain* is timely when the numbers of children on the move across Europe is increasing by the tens of thousands per year. The accounts shared bring the life-changing nature of these experiences into sharp focus and the need to ensure they do not have to deal with their trauma alone. This book also provides such inspiration and focus for professionals to look within, around, and to question and act.

I would recommend all social workers, social work managers, directors and policymakers read this book and be reminded that each and every one of them is pivotal in addressing these issues as we grapple with this complex and deeply disturbing problem of our time.

# Preface

As a social worker, I've worked with many young refugees and asylum seekers over the years, many of whom I have got to know really well and have respected and liked. When I reflect on this group of young people, I greatly admire how they have overcome many struggles and tribulations, and how many of them have turned into well-adjusted young people with the potential to achieve great things in life. I have never met nicer or more capable young people in my career than this group. But these young people have suffered greatly. Young asylum seekers have a much better understanding of the world and how it works than citizen children, and indeed their life experiences often defy those of many adults. Their suffering and endurance are sometimes beyond our capacity to understand.

An ex-client telephoned me one day in a state of panic about the coronavirus. It was still in its early stages and the possibility of lockdown was not mentioned, but the young person had seen internet coverage and spoken with friends, which had escalated his anxiety about catching the virus. His friends thought he was taking it far too seriously. He was unable to sleep at night and as the numbers of people contracting the disease increased, along with the death toll, his fear intensified even further, resulting in him ringing me daily for reassurance. He continuously asked what he should do to keep safe and wondered if he would survive if he became infected. He even stopped smoking because he feared his lungs wouldn't cope with the virus.

While I gave him advice on how to protect himself, it didn't automatically register with me what was truly going on in his mind at first. Yes, he was stressed, anxious and overthinking the situation, but then I realised this was primarily caused by traumatic flashbacks to his past. Here was a young man who had grown up in war-torn Iraq and had regularly witnessed death before experiencing the gruelling journey to Britain. Coronavirus became a reminder of his loss and led to his anxiety around the deaths of people in his life and the possibility that further people he knew would die here in Britain. In this book, I have included a full chapter about trauma and the impact it has on young people, who sometimes receive little empathy or help to cope with their emotional distress.

The main reason I wrote this book was to highlight the unfair treatment and sometimes lack of resources and services available to young people in this country. Equally, however, I wanted to illustrate the good practice that takes place. I wanted to dispel the misconceptions that mainstream society and some professionals, including social workers, often hold about this group. As a social worker myself, I am fully aware of the limitations of the role. Admittedly, social workers have to adhere to budget restrictions, resources and managerial direction, but that can never be an excuse for lacking compassion or the giving of time and professional friendship.

In the book of prose and poetry entitled *Teaching My Mother How to Give Birth*, Warsan Shire (2011, p 26) sums up the harshness of refugee life in a very profound way.

*I know a few things to be true. I do not know where I am going, where I have come from is disappearing. I am unwelcome and my beauty is not beauty here. My body is burning with the shame of not belonging, my body is longing. I am the sin of memory. I watch the news and my mouth becomes a sink full of blood. The lines, the forms, the people at the desks, the calling cards, the immigration officer, the looks on the streets, the cold settling into my bones, the English classes at night, the distance I am from home.*

Social workers need to have the ability to make young people feel valued and respected, and to encourage their rich diversity to come shining through by making them realise the value that it brings to our society. The ability to boost their self-confidence and self-worth by acknowledging young people's strengths and talents should be a mandatory part of the job.

While the reader will see that young people in the care system and care leavers receive a better service than young adult asylum seekers first arriving in Britain after the age of 18, that does not mean they are highly advantaged. Admittedly, there are benefits to being a child in care or a care leaver. However, placing young people in sparsely furnished shared independent accommodation without even a television, or expecting them to survive on a £120 a year clothing allowance, as some local authorities do, is unjustifiable. Young adult asylum seekers who are not care leavers have anything but an easy time. Without help from charities or the kindness of individuals, many would become lost in profound poverty and desperate loneliness. Even with the help they receive, some of them without refugee status live a pitiful existence.

This book is mainly aimed at professionals and will be of particular benefit to social work students and social workers who work with young asylum seekers and refugees. Increasing understanding, sharing background stories and reasons for asylum, and highlighting the services and resources available ensures this book will also prove useful to psychology students, teachers and college tutors too. The general public who wish to learn more about the plight of asylum seekers will also find much of interest in this book. There are plenty of people in Britain who live in nice areas, own nice houses and earn nice salaries who could not care less about refugees or social justice – but equally there are many people who are interested and show a good moral conscience.

I make no apology for accusing the social work profession of mainly being voiceless. I dislike the cowardice of not speaking publicly about injustices and poor services. I question where its integrity and duty of care lie, and whether it remains silent to cover up its own inadequacies. I will leave it to the reader to determine whether some of those responsible for caring for the most vulnerable in our society are no different from some in the general populace, with the nice jobs and salaries, who don't care about the hardships and difficulties faced by refugees and asylum seekers. In the end, is it not a matter of conscience and good moral fibre that makes a difference? It wouldn't be unjust to say that, based on my research and interviews, a lack of conscience exists in the government, scaling downwards from the Home Office to local authorities, managers and social workers. It is my hope that this book serves to highlight injustices in the refugee and asylum arena that I believe deserve greater attention before many more young people are let down by this country.

# Acknowledgements

There are a great number of people who I consulted during my research that deservedly need thanking – I only wish I had kept a better note of those who gave up their valuable time and shared their expertise with me. After trawling through saved emails in an attempt to ensure that nobody gets left out, I can only apologise if I miss somebody's name.

I would like to say thank you to the following people for their time and knowledge: Razia Shariff – CEO at Kent Refugee Action Network; Alex Hillier at Kent Kindness; Claire Murphy, Neil Thayne and Helen Johnson at the Refugee Council; Dane Buckley at the UK Lesbian & Gay Immigration Group; Lauren Scott at Refugees At Home; Lilian Simonsson at Enthum Foundation in Eastbourne; Marian Spiers at the Dost Centre in London; Renuka Jeyarajah-Dent at Coram; Lucy Williams at the University of Kent; Nick Watts at Together Migrant Children; Philip Ishola at Love 146 (author of the personal endorsement to this book); Kelly Devenney at the University of York; Eleanor Brown at Community Action for Refugees and Asylum Seekers in London; Helen Cullen at Asylum Welcome; Rosie Rooney at Safe Passage; and Jovana Fordham and Ben Jenkins at the British Red Cross.

I would also like to thank individuals who had knowledge of refugees and asylum seekers from having worked with them previously and to those currently working with them, who spoke to me in their own private capacity while not representing any particular local authority or charitable organisation. These include: Nick Crick, Farman Rustem, Mario Silva, Issa Olwengo and Anne Nolan.

Special thanks to Rozalina Dimitrova-Semerdjieva, Anita Kimber and Mark Williams from London South East College Plumstead for allowing me to meet with young refugees and asylum seekers on the Entry Level 3 ESOL course. I met with the young people for the best part of an academic term and it was here that the creative stories contained in Chapter 6 Voices of Young People were birthed.

Thank you to Brian Bilston for his kind permission in allowing his poem 'Refugees' to be used.

I would also like to pay tribute to all of the young people who contributed their stories or had some verbal input into my research. The bravery and resilience of these young people was very humbling, but their enthusiasm, ambition and good humour was heart-warming.

Many thanks to my contacts in Istanbul – Abdullah Taomh for sharing his story and Basak Erpolat at the Syrian Cultural Centre. Thanks are also due to contacts in the Republic of Ireland for their time and input – including Robert King at Spirasi in Dublin and James Gannon at Refugee Support Ballahaderreen in County Roscommon.

I would also like to say a special thank you to Lord Alfred Dubs who graciously gave of his time to meet with me – and who has written a Foreword at the beginning of this book.

Last but by no means least, let me say a big thank you to Di Page – director at Critical Publishing – and her team, for all their wonderful guidance and support.

# Introduction

There are millions of displaced young people across the world that have fled war zones, persecution and poverty. For many years, those seeking shelter in the UK have been given a largely negative press and that includes UASC (unaccompanied asylum-seeking children), a large percentage of whom have come from Sudan, Eritrea, Vietnam, Albania, Iraq, Iran, Afghanistan, Ethiopia and Syria. Despite entering a life of uncertainty, often with a suspended future, and haunted by memories, these young people strive to make Britain their home as they navigate their way through the unfamiliar mires of Children's Services, legal professionals and the Home Office.

Young asylum seekers often lose some of their original personality during the ordeal of getting to the UK. However, despite this, and regardless of having no direct family support through these formative years of their lives, they do their best to learn English and make Britain their new home. As you will learn from this chapter, life in Britain can be tough for these young people. At some point they will realise the part their parents have played in their plight by paying smugglers to get them to the UK, despite the huge risk and ever-increasingly complex border crossings. Securing Leave to Remain (LTR) status becomes harder and harder. Some young people may even be forced into being dishonest, which is often contrary to their nature. However, statistically, few enter the criminal justice system.

# Dreaming of home

Little background history is sometimes known about the pre-departure lives of young asylum seekers and refugees. They are often an enigma. Sometimes they fear revealing too much about their backgrounds because they have been instructed by agents to reveal little and only when necessary. However, it must be noted that they also get caught up in a system that does not care a great deal about their earlier life experiences and how this might impact their new lives in the UK. Some parts of their earlier years will be obliterated, particularly for those young people who fled countries with their parents and siblings at short notice, only to become separated during the journey. Most do not have a single photograph to remind them of their family.

Some talk about wanting to return home one day when their country of origin settles and is considered safe. Others realise this will never be possible, because to do so would carry the risk of prosecution and imprisonment. Some young people understand they are displaced away from their origins and that they must find a sense of belonging elsewhere. For those awaiting refugee status, they remain wondering where and what will happen to them if they fail to get their papers. They live in limbo and know only struggle and isolation, but this might not always be obvious at first sight. Young people surround themselves with other young people. Camaraderie and laughter are common sights when they are with friends but, as one young person told me, the thought of returning home at night to a house where there is no family and no welcome is a painful reminder of what is missing and what they have to endure.

# Reasons for asylum

The reasons why young asylum seekers come to Europe and the UK have not changed greatly over the past 20 years. A minority are still escaping poverty and their journeys here are fraught with many dangers and hardships. There are also a minority who are trafficked. The majority, however, still arrive because of political reasons and/or to escape war and conflict, as opposed to economic reasons. There is clear evidence that these young people come from families who have had enough wealth to pay agents to smuggle them out of the country. Most young people are aware of the deals struck by their parents and agents, but rarely mention this to professionals. Agents firmly warn young people to never discuss the full extent of their lives, the finer details that fall outside the 'thin' story they are furnished with and instructed to learn and regurgitate to border agencies, the police, Home Office officials and social workers. This 'thin' story that will outline the reason why they are seeking asylum will include an element of truth but not be entirely honest. Bearing this in mind, it is not fair to dismiss these young people as liars without realising that they are a victim of a system they were forced into, one that was outside of their own personal control.

Young asylum seekers and refugees carry several burdens around with them. The psychological effects of having to leave their homelands and families at the behest of their parents are quite complex. On the one hand, they are made to feel loved and special, hence why they were chosen as the family member to leave. This often leaves the young person feeling obliged to create a successful life because of the financial sacrifices that their parents made, despite the many obstacles they face for several years after they have left their country. On the other hand, they feel guilt at being the ones who escaped the war and suffering while their parents and siblings remained behind and were still exposed to life-threatening situations. Then there is the promise of family reunification, which seldom materialises and if/when it does is often not as treasured as expected. The simple fact is that when a young person leaves their home-land, they adjust to a new culture and grow roots that are very different to those of their original homeland. This mentally changes young people and their outlooks on life, resulting in further guilt and often shame when displeasure and rejection sets in as they compare their new life to their 'old' one.

# Myths and misconceptions

When a person gets to know or befriends a refugee or asylum seeker, they begin to think more positively of them and, as a result, they automatically find them less 'threatening'. They see that they are human beings with the same needs, likes, dislikes and ambitions as themselves. That is why young refugees need to be part of the com-munity – in schools, colleges and youth centres – and should not be segregated from others. This way, their differences are reduced. Although this sounds idealistic, it doesn't have to be. Unfortunately, there is still a lot of misinformation in society about refugees and the reasons why people seek asylum, including the following.

» People have listened to politicians who question whether young asylum seekers are genuine or bogus and if they have come here for a better life. This doubt has grown among the general public, even though there is no evidence that this is true.

» There is a dichotomy in the press, with some broadsheets portraying images of the 'poor' refugee, while tabloids portray them as liars/criminals. The human child gets lost in the middle of this.

» Some people believe they are criminals who come here for free housing and to cheat the benefits system. Any males over the age of 16 are viewed as 'young men'. They are seen in the streets where they are often loud and bois-terous. As a society, we are often intimidated by them. Some people question why those seeking asylum are being supported over UK citizen children.

» Other people believe that young asylum seekers have no reason to be in the UK and have come here to exploit, enjoy an easy life and take full advantage of free handouts.

» Another belief is that young people come to the UK for free accommodation. There is a misconception that they take the good places to live, as well as taking jobs away from British citizens. (The truth is that most are exploited with cash-in-hand jobs.)

» There is little understanding of the suffering they endured during their journey. Some spend up to two years travelling and suffer huge trauma.

» Some people believe that some young asylum seekers are terrorists sent here by ISIS – that they are dangerous and must be avoided. (There is no evidence that any of this is true.)

» Others believe they lie about their age. This is because a few have been highlighted in the media as being older than they claimed.

» People question why young people passed through several countries and didn't claim asylum. They do not realise that most of these countries, including Greece and Italy, hold a hostile attitude towards refugees.

» An assumption is often made that they all come under the umbrella of economic migrants from Eastern Europe (like Slovakia and Poland). Many believe they have come to the UK and taken advantage of social housing and/or are given jobs instead of UK citizens.

» The word 'refugee' is often used as a general word or description in reference to a whole mix of people living in the UK who were not born here and whose first language is other than English. It is often used in an ill-informed way, but is not always meant as a racist slur.

There is a poem entitled 'Refugees'* by Brian Bilston, which offers perhaps the best opportunity to see both sides of the refugee debate. Here, the perspective of those who are anti-immigration through ignorance, prejudice and discrimination is easily tipped to the other side by those not opposed to it and who show understanding, compassion and a willingness to help.

# Refugees

*They have no need of our help*
*So do not tell me*
*These haggard faces could belong to you or me*
*Should life have dealt a different hand*
*We need to see them for who they really are*
*Chancers and scroungers*
*Layabouts and loungers*
*With bombs up their sleeves*
*Cut-throats and thieves*
*They are not*
*Welcome here*

---

* Taken from *Voices of Culture*, capturing the core themes of the conference *The Role of Culture in Promoting Inclusion in the Context of Migration* that was held on 14–15 June 2016, in Brussels, representing the cultural sectors from the EU member states.

*We should make them*
*Go back to where they came from*
*They cannot*
*Share our food*
*Share our homes*
*Share our countries*
*Instead let us*
*Build a wall to keep them out*
*It is not okay to say*
*These are people just like us*
*A place should only belong to those who are born there*
*Do not be so stupid to think that*
*The world can be looked at another way*
*(now read from bottom to top)*

# Definitions

The words 'asylum seeker' and 'refugee' are sometimes used interchangeably although there is a distinct difference in their respective meaning.

## Asylum seeker

An asylum seeker is somebody – adult or child – who flees their homeland and makes themselves known to the authorities after they arrive in another country. Once they have submitted an asylum application, they have a legal right to stay in the country until the Home Office decides whether to grant them asylum. The Home Office (2017, p 13) have defined an unaccompanied minor as follows.

*An unaccompanied asylum-seeking child is a person who, at the time of making the asylum application, is or (if there is no proof) appears to be under 18; is applying for asylum in his or her own right; and has no adult relatives or guardian to turn to in this country.*

## Refugee

A refugee is somebody – adult or child – who has proven to the Home Office that they would be at risk if they returned to their home country and are therefore granted LTR. A refugee can also be described as somebody who – owing to a well-rounded fear of being persecuted for reasons of race, religion, nationality, membership of a particular social group or political opinion – is outside the country of their nationality and is unable, or owing to such a fear is unwilling, to avail of the protection of that country.

Somebody who is a refuge may have submitted a claim for international protection under the United Nations (UN) Refugee Convention 1951, where under Article 15c there is: *'A serious and individual threat to a civilian's life or person by reason of indiscriminative violence in situations of international or internal armed conflict.'* In the UK, this also covers a claim for 'humanitarian protection' where the person – adult or child – has passed the legal test that confirmed that substantial grounds have been shown for believing that the person concerned faces a real risk of being subjected to torture or to inhumane or degrading treatment or punishment in the country if the person is returned.

# Countries of origin

The following is a list of countries where most young people who are seeking asylum in the UK come from, with the key reasons why they may have had to leave their countries.

## Afghanistan

Political unrest. Persistent violence by militia and Islamist groups. Forced conscription of young males. Exploitation and trafficking of young people, including organ harvesting.

## Albania

Large-scale trafficking and exploitation of young men, mainly by violent drug dealers. Widespread poverty and unemployment. Economic migration in the hope of a better life.

## Eritrea

Dictatorship country with forced conscription of young males. Profound poverty and slave labour and maltreatment of its people. Female genital mutilation carried out.

## Ethiopia

Political unrest and persecution among the Oromo population. Political persecution. Ongoing drought, coupled with seasonal floods. High levels of poverty.

## Iran

Conflict between religious groups and the persecution of Christians. Widespread persecution of political activists. Murder of gay men and maltreatment of the wider LGBT community.

## Iraq

Political unrest and violence following years of war. Young men forced into militias. Islamist terrorism. Religious intolerance of Christians. Ethnic persecution of the Kurdish community.

## Sudan

Political persecution. Violence and destruction by ethnicity and religion in civil war (south of the country) over many decades. Islamist terrorism. Widespread poverty.

## Somalia

Catastrophic famine and widespread drought. Ethnic conflict, Islamist terrorism, violence and political unrest. Female genital mutilation. Little hope for the future.

## Syria

Destruction of the country as a result of civil war. Widespread ethnic and religious violence in the civil war by government and non-government forces. Islamist terrorism.

## Vietnam

Exploitation and escaping trafficking. Religious persecution between Buddhists and Christian and religious sects. Poverty and economic deprivation.

# Immigration status

On average, approximately 25,000 asylum seekers arrive in the UK each year (significantly less than those arriving in Germany, Italy and France). This includes between 2000 and 3000 young people who turn up annually without parents or guardians. Many will have crossed the Channel to the UK in small boats, because the safe routes have been tightened and they are only left with this dangerous option. A third of these young people will be given refugee status or humanitarian protection. Many will wait over a year before their Home Office interview and over 40 per cent will wait a further six months post-interview for initial rulings to be made. If the outcome is negative, the decision may then be challenged in court. The majority of those who are initially unsuccessful usually go down this route. Around a third of appeals are allowed, in effect overturning the Home Office's initial decision. Kent cares for a fifth of Britain's unaccompanied under-18s. Other councils with large numbers of asylum-seeking young people include Croydon, Surrey, Essex, Thurrock and Islington.

There is a difference between failure and success. Those who are given LTR status flourish more easily – their worries are instantly lessened. They become more settled and secure. There are fewer mental health concerns and they can focus better on their education. Failure to secure LTR status, however, often leads to the opposite outcome, coupled with segregation from those with status who can move forward with their resettlement and lives.

Many young people struggle. Africans coming here see their journey as their rite of passage. It is expected of them and viewed within their society as something that should happen. For some, this is an adventure, pioneering out into the big wide world – becoming a man – before the harsh reality that life in the UK is not as easy or straightforward as they had imagined. Those from Iraq and Afghanistan struggle more because their departure is often unexpected, especially the younger ones who end up very confused about their situation. They have had to escape from their country at short notice.

Placing young people where they would ideally like to live continuously proves to be problematic, not least those placed with affluent foster carers in rural areas resulting in many requesting to move because they feel they are '*the only person*' in their area/neighbourhood. They want to live where '*people like them live*', be able to easily access food establishments and shops, and to mix with peers from their countries of origin with the same culture and language.

# Iranian asylum seekers

Young asylum seekers from Iran fear they may be viewed as economic migrants based on comments from the Home Secretary's office that stated that powers would be deployed to ensure those seeking asylum would not be successful in their claims. This, combined with hostile news headlines about young Iranians crossing the English Channel in small boats, has resulted in headlines warning of a migrant invasion. This contrasts greatly to expatriate Iranians living in the UK since the 1979 revolution.

When they came to the UK in the late 1970s and early 1980s, they experienced a lot of understanding and empathy from Home Office officials who were known to visit them in refugee centres at the time, as opposed to expecting them to visit their office.

These days, young people arriving in the UK from Iran are often fleeing vulnerable, chaotic and tragic situations. They are not self-sufficient and do not come from educated backgrounds. The majority who flee Iran have experienced poverty and lived under the shadow of violence, especially if their parents have tried to earn an income outside of the system in the vain attempt of making a living.

I spoke to a 17-year-old male who fled Iran after his father was imprisoned for smuggling alcohol across the border between Iraq and Iran. He was implicated too, because he had helped his father. The youngster would get up at 4am every day and he and his father would walk their horse, which was used for carrying goods, across the mountain terrain before crossing the border into Iraq, taking care not to be detected by border police. There, his father would buy alcohol to sell back in Iran and then they would resume their journey back home. It was an arduous task that took up to 14 hours to complete. When they got home they had dinner before going to bed to rest in preparation for repeating the long journey the next day. They did these trips four or five times a week, until one day the police received a tip-off. The young man said his father was imprisoned and he fears he may never be released. He may even be hanged for what he did. Afterwards, the young person fled Iran for his safety, knowing that if he didn't the police may come and arrest him too.

The young man's story reminded me of something that happened at a day centre I visited for young asylum seekers and refugees. A team member raised two valuable points relating to the plight of the young people they helped. He asked, '*Do we really know what they have been through and do we really know what they left behind?*' The answer is clearly '*no*' to both, because there is no way of knowing how much hardship, loss and uncertainty these young people have suffered. The only certainty is knowing that all of them will have experienced suffering at some point or other in their young lives.

Iranian young people arrive in the UK with fears and experiences vastly different from those of indigenous children. The young person I spoke to told me that nobody is allowed to have a girlfriend in public in Iran, otherwise they risk getting murdered either by the girl's family or the authorities. Sex outside of marriage is a great taboo, yet many young people risk their lives to have secret sex. Drinking alcohol is heavily punishable, with those found guilty often being imprisoned for a month. Heavy drug misuse can result in the death penalty. Life is strict and the poorer you are the stricter it is because those on low incomes are unable to bribe their way out of trouble.

# Afrim (17) from Albania

*Afrim's parents only knew he was on his way to the UK when he telephoned them from France. He planned his escape from Albania two months before he left. He said he had to get out of the country because the future offered him nothing. His father was disabled after losing a hand in an accident, resulting in him being long-term unemployed. Afrim's mother suffered from depression and stayed in for days or weeks at a time, withdrawn from the world. His two older brothers tried to work whenever offered casual waitering jobs, but opportunities were rare and wages low.*

*Afrim liked school but knew that there was no worthwhile future for him in Albania. He felt that his good command of English would be the gateway towards building a new life in Britain, so he set out on his journey travelling first to Italy then France before going to Belgium, from where he commenced the final leg of his journey to Dover. He arrived in the back of a lorry with three other young males. Afrim said he will always remember the moment he got out of the lorry and was able to breathe properly after being enclosed in a compartment with little oxygen for four hours. He also urgently wanted to go to the toilet but was told by a police officer that he would have to wait.*

*Afrim feels happy living in the UK. He wants to go to college and build a positive future for himself. He dreams of getting a good job that will enable him to send money home to his parents and brothers. Afrim doesn't miss Albania, where people used to refer to him and his family as 'Pakuks' – a derogatory term used to condemn somebody who is so poor they are unable to even buy bread. Afrim said that 70 per cent of Albanians are poor. He isn't keen on his religion either. He was born Muslim but has never practised. He knows little about the prophet Mohammad and has never read the Qur'an. He acknowledges that 65 per cent of people are Muslim in Albania, but few remain true to their religion.*

*Although Afrim is optimistic about the future, he is also realistic. He has two uncles who live in the UK, but he says he doesn't want any contact with them and won't ask for their help. He explains that his Albanian pride prevents him from doing so. For the time being, he lives for the moment. He is enjoying making new friends, watching films and meeting girls. Afrim freely states that although life in Britain is far from perfect, it is still ten times better than life in Albania could ever be. But he realises his chances of getting status are slim and feels that Britain does not fully understand that drug-related gangs and criminal blood-fuelled killings are rife in Albania, making many young people fearful of their lives.*

# African asylum seekers

Asylum seekers come to the UK from various parts of Africa, but in my experience the four main countries are Eritrea, Sudan, Somalia and Ethiopia. Each country is different in terms of history and culture, although each share their own historical suffering and brutality – which still continues to the present day. Poverty, war, dictatorship, genocide and terrorism have drained these countries of their life force, thus eluding peace and economic prosperity for millions of innocent people who have either fled the oppression, are displaced among it, or exist in misery and hardship.

Eritrea, which has been under the dictatorship of President Isaias Aferki since 1993, is highly militarised and constantly preoccupied by the threat of war with Ethiopia. Eritrea and Ethiopia were a colony of the kingdom of Italy until 1936, when Mussolini brought profound changes to the colonial government in Eritrea that eventually led to independence between the two countries. Eritrea is a multi-religious country – split in two, with almost an equal percentage of its citizens either being Orthodox Christian or Muslim. It is one of the most isolated and repressive countries in the world, and remains one of the poorest in Africa.

The majority of young African asylum seekers come from Eritrea, where thousands flee mandatory army conscription, believing they have no future. Their choice is to undertake compulsory national service or try to flee. Eritrea's national service is harsh, pays a pittance and goes on indefinitely. Stories are often told of young men forced into this harsh regime having to share a dorm with up to 200 others, spend a year in the desert and being forbidden to contact family members for several years. Usually, conscripts go into the military. The thought of this hellish life of long hours, boredom, malnutrition and inhumane conditions means that most young Eritreans flee their homeland to escape.

Ethiopia, on the other hand, which is mainly Orthodox Christian (approximately 10 per cent are Muslim), has one of the fastest growing economies in Africa. It is also one of the safest to visit. The population is very diverse and made up of 80 different ethnic groups. However, the Oromo tribe, situated in central Ethiopia, a culture with its own language and religion, consists of 25 million people (a third of the population) and is the largest and most discriminated against of all the tribal ethnic groups. Political unrest has blighted this region of Ethiopia for a very long time, with century-old roots, but ultimately this ongoing human rights issue can be viewed as an ethnic cleansing of the Oromo people who inhabit Ethiopia. An armed conflict between the OLF (Oromo Liberation Front) and the Ethiopian government has seen thousands flee the region for their safety because they are often targeted by security forces in violent land-grabbing coups. Persecutions are commonplace, along with the burning down of entire villages and the massacring of inhabitants. Overall, it is estimated that several hundred thousand people have been displaced as a result of this brutal and ongoing conflict.

Sudan is a complex country and must be seen as two separate countries – South and North. South Sudan is officially known as the Republic of South Sudan, having gained independence from the Republic of Sudan (North Sudan) in 2011. South Sudan is one of the poorest and most violent countries in Africa and has the worst social and economic indicators in the world. It consists of Christian and Animist people who, for decades, struggled against the Arab Muslim rule in the north of the country, which consisted of genocide and attacks by armed militia but eventually led to independence. Despite independence from each other, both South and North have unresolved issues around shared oil revenues and border demarcation, which continues to create tensions.

The death toll in Sudan (as a result of genocide and armed militia conflict) over the last ten years has exceeded two million. Several million are internally displaced, while others have fled to neighbouring countries, including Eritrea and Somalia. A large percentage of Sudanese young people claiming asylum in the UK, however, come from Darfur, a western part of the Republic of Sudan (North Sudan) where rebel groups cause civil unrest and violence over land disputes and water access. North Sudan is mainly Muslim and considered far safer, peaceful and more tolerant than South Sudan, but nevertheless this armed conflict – and what some consider to be genocide – has resulted in thousands of deaths and has made Darfur and its surrounding regions an extremely dangerous place. There are more than 1.4 million displaced people living in camps in Darfur who rely on food handouts. Many others have fled the country.

Somalia, which is mainly a Muslim country, is one of the most violent in Africa and among the ten poorest countries in the world. Forty-three per cent of the population live in extreme poverty and over half the labour force is unemployed. The main source of livelihood is livestock management. It has poor health services, inadequate sanitation and a life expectancy of just over the age of 50 because of the high number of fatal infectious diseases. A civil war started in the country in 2009 between the government and Al-Shabaab, an Islamist terrorist group that is linked to Al-Qaeda. Al-Shabaab is the largest militant organisation and it aims to oust the Somali government from power. The group seeks to establish a new Somalia state, ruled according to its strict interpretation of Sharia law. Its quest to do so has resulted in daily chaos and suffering, with routine kidnappings, armed conflict and violent crime. Ultimately, this violence has destroyed the country and the war has (so far) resulted in the Somali people being scattered in their millions to refugee camps and neighbouring countries (including Kenya and Yemen) and in their hundreds of thousands to other parts of the world, including the UK.

## Yonas (16) from Eritrea

*After I left, my mother sat in the house refusing to go outside. She cried every day and nobody could console her. Occasionally, we get to speak on the telephone, but she continuously asks me if I am okay and if I am safe. She knows little about Britain and can't imagine living in a country with rights and freedom. Few people have rights back home – only the president and his family. Everybody over 18 in Eritrea must join the army if they do not go on into higher education after secondary school. Leaving school earlier than 18 means you must join the army sooner, because anybody over the age of 13 can be called up for duty.*

*I was clever at school but had to stop going when I was 14 because my father fell ill. He got an infection in his foot and was unable to look after our goats, which were our main source of livelihood. I had intended going back after his foot got better, but by then I had been reported to the authorities for not attending school. Maybe they thought I had stopped for good. The army sent a letter telling me I had to join. I dreaded the prospect of this. After you enter the army, you are only allowed home to visit your family once every two years. I had little time to make up my mind, but I decided to leave Eritrea. I miss my family terribly and worry so much about them. But I am one of the lucky ones who made it to the UK alive and well. Some of my friends died during sea crossings or in the desert as they made their way by foot across Ethiopia and Sudan and Libya.*

# Kurdish asylum seekers

Kurdistan is a mountainous region of southwest Asia spread throughout the boundaries of four countries (population figures are approximate): Turkey (with a Kurd population of 14–15 million), Iran (8–9 million), Iraq (6–7 million) and Syria (2–3 million). Kurds are largely Sunni Muslim people, with their own language and culture. They have endured decades of suffering, genocide and brutality, mainly at the hands of Iraq, and consider themselves as having been lied to and cheated by the West. Some Kurds believe that the western world helped create the ideology that formed terrorist groups like ISIS in Iraq and Syria, which have deeply affected their people. Kurds have many good qualities that are easily recognised. They are brave, friendly and warm-hearted people, with beautiful jovial natures making them easy to like. They are well-mannered, too, and respect others – especially women and elders.

It is estimated that approximately 80 per cent of young Kurdish people claiming asylum in the UK come from comfortable and sometimes rich families – which has allowed their journeys to Europe and the UK to be funded. Most will have enjoyed a good lifestyle, holidays and material items, despite living in a country affected by corruption, war, bloodshed and brutality that has sadly become a way of life for millions. Approximately 30 per cent of older young people will have driven their own cars, and many will have been accustomed to security and servants in their family homes. There will be some Kurds, though, without these affluent backgrounds who have made their way to the UK thanks to determination, resourcefulness and being able to obtain financial assistance through corrupt means. Some will have fled because of fear of honour killings after it was found they had a girlfriend and/or had sex outside marriage or impregnated a girl. Others get involved in oppositional political parties, where punishments are severe for those who openly protest.

All of these young people will, however, have come here because they have no future back home. Their families fear for their safety, as well as feeling that they have no long-term prospects. Here are parents who want to project their children into a safer, more secure country than the one they live in. Of course, this is not only indicative of Kurdish parents, but rather a general commonality among all parents from troubled countries wanting a better life for their child. But in Iraq, Iran and Syria, the political situation can change at any time. Families have endured decades of upheaval and unrest. Those living in Iraq fear another Saddam Hussein can come into power at any moment – or that a further terrorist group like ISIS can take root. Kurds have survived ethnic cleansing and other brutality under Saddam's regime and feel exhausted and worn out by bloodshed. The overall general feeling is that things will not get better because nobody trusts the system or the government.

While waiting for the Home Office decisions, Kurdish young people are not unlike others, with many getting on with life while others drift along in a sullen, reclusive and confused way. Others feel liberation when they enter a new society and want to enjoy it to the full, and they may feel held back by foster carers and social workers or anybody else who places rules and boundaries on their lives. Some young people prefer to focus on the 'here and now', which often means leaving the past behind. It can only be surmised that this may impact on them emotionally later in life. The fact remains however, as Kohli (2006) points out, that asylum seekers and refugees will miss their families along with the sights, sounds, smells and textures of living in their childhood environments. Indeed, young Kurds often mention that their country is full of beautiful rugged mountains, valleys and meadows.

All asylum seekers come with 'thin' stories and 'thick' stories. The thin story is the fabricated account of their lives, while the thick story is the truth. Help is given by agents, smugglers, family members and other young people within their community to devise a story that will be acceptable to the Home Office for an asylum claim to be successful. The consensus is that real stories are not believed or would cause trouble if divulged. Therefore, it is considered better to invent a story that is hard or impossible to prove. Young people fear not being believed – even those who come from Syria where they have escaped or witnessed torture, mental and physical suffering, with many themselves having sustained injuries. Often in the asylum-seeking arena, the Home Office is viewed as being unsophisticated, with many people even considering it stupid. So, it is considered easier and more productive to embellish the truth or create a story that is completely different to the truth.

Some young asylum seekers even deliberately fail to divulge details about family members who may live in other parts of the UK. Indeed, it is from these family sources that these young people are often given mobile phones, clothes and money. It is thought that only a quarter of young people will use their real names, but even those who do will use a shortened version. Overall, it is estimated that three-quarters will use a totally fabricated name, and everybody will use a false date of birth. It is incredible to think that this level of dishonesty is needed in order to seek safety and protection. Why the Home Office demands these lengthy stories, rather than concentrating on the unsafe nature of the countries the young person has escaped from, needs to be questioned.

## Kassim (17) from Iraq

*Whispers had begun to circulate. Kassim and his girlfriend had been seeing each other in secret and believed their romance lay undetected. That was until one day when they were in a town away from their home area, away from their school and friends, and some elders from their community spotted them and reported this back to the girl's parents. The girl made some excuse, but suspicions had been aroused.*

*Kassim continued to see his girlfriend and one day they drove to a secluded place and had sex in the car. When the mother found blood on the girl's underwear, she confronted her, and the girl confessed under pressure. It was decided retribution had to be sought for this sin, which was blamed on Kassim's inability to curtail his emotions. The girl's parents deemed her maimed and loathed Kassim for stealing her virginity. Justice was required for what the Holy Qur'an considered a grave sin. Kassim would have to pay with his life for the harm he had done. Nothing would compensate for the damage caused. No apology, no matter how well meaning, would suffice. No financial settlement, no matter how generous, would be enough to alleviate the shame and hurt. The girl's parents could never see life returning to normal ever again. Kassim's death was the only thing that seemed agreeable to help manage their pain.*

*Word got through to Kassim's family about what the girl's family were planning. His father knew of similar incidents where killings took place and so he took the threats seriously. He instantly put Kassim in hiding, partly because he thought things might quieten down if he went and spoke directly to the family. Money was offered and declined. The threats continued and assurances were given that a price had been put on Kassim's head for his capture and killing. He would never be safe if he returned home. His death card was marked and the only way to unmark it was to leave the country. One night, shortly afterwards, Kassim was taken to the border and under the cover of darkness met with the agent who had agreed a price with his father to get him out of the country. And so Kassim began his journey, one that would take him to Europe before finally arriving several months later in Dover in the back of a lorry, along with six other young males of similar age to himself.*

Asylum-seeking young people in the UK soon discover they are unable to talk openly about their previous lives – rather they must guard the secrecy of their past. Stories and lives only become visible after they have become asylum seekers, with professionals unable or unwilling to devote more time into seeking information about their lives in their homelands. They are rarely viewed as multi-dimensional – ie family, culture and desires are rooted in another country, rather than merely focusing on their lives in the present form with little or no regard for their past. This approach means that only the briefest snippets of the 'real' child or young person are revealed. Whoever they are or wherever they have come from, they are still young people who must leave their homelands for their long-term safety and, as a result, deserve to be treated as children in need.

The over-riding impression that I personally formed of Kurdish young people who I worked with is that they are hard-working. They like to find employment and earn their own money and do not wish to rely on the welfare state. In my opinion, they have the best work ethic that I have witnessed among young refugees. However, insiders from the Kurdish community have spoken about fellow Kurds having extravagant tastes, being materialistically minded and money focused. They were of the impression that some of their community feel 'outsiders' in Britain and desire to be as rich as, if not richer than, the 'insider' – ie a British person born here – to prove they are equally as good as them. It was also acknowledged that some young adult Kurds are given money from their families to start businesses such as barber shops and mobile phone shops. I need to point out that while this viewpoint has come from various sources within the Kurdish community, it is anecdotal and that there is currently no statistical evidence that indicates that Kurdish people are either more successful or less successful than any other nationality of refugee in the UK.

## Kamran (16) from Iraq

*Kamran kept going to college, hoping that his social worker would one day ring him with good news from the Home Office. He learned to speak good English, because he felt it was very important for a good life in Britain. He wanted to learn a skill or trade and hoped to get a good job after he finished college. He said he knows he would never be able to be like other indigenous young people of his age and would never become a doctor or a teacher. He felt he would never get that chance because of his background and the lack of earlier education in his country.*

*Kamran considers Britain to be safe for refugees if a person keeps their head down and avoids getting into trouble. He said, though, that he was in a cafe one evening when a man came up to him and offered to pay him between £50 and £70 a day if he answered a mobile phone for him. All Kamran would have to do was answer the phone and give a name or address or something to whoever called. Kamran told the man he wasn't interested but, before the man left, he tried again to persuade him by telling him that if he did what he was asked then Kamran would be able to live in a nice house and have nice clothes. The man also told Kamran that he would get him nice girls for sex if he worked for him.*

*Kamran believes the prime minister should change the asylum system in the UK and make Britain a much better place for refugees. He said he currently lives in a town where the authorities have housed far too many refugees. Kamran said that English people don't understand asylum seekers. He said the majority don't know the difference between migrants and refugees, and he often finds people staring at him and his friends as if they are not human, that they are monsters. There is also racist name calling or people mumbling at them under their breath. He said he hates having to live like this.*

# Vietnamese asylum seekers

The cost of a young person leaving Vietnam to come to Europe and the UK, most of whom are male, is estimated to be approximately £40,000 – half to get to Europe and a further half to reach the UK. Many people in Vietnam know of families who benefit from having relatives in the UK because they regularly send back money. Therefore, they believe the high cost and risks are worth the potential reward.

There are massive numbers of people who want to make a new life. Parents are easily manipulated by sophisticated traffickers and their brokers. They desperately want something better than what their Vietnamese life offers, and have the idea that their lives are going to change for the better. They think this will be an investment for future generations of their family – a long-term investment, but money well spent. They ignore all the danger and the warning signs presented to them by the government, media and friends.

Young people endure long ordeals. They are held for months at a time with other migrants in squalid, crowded basements in Russia, the Ukraine and the Czech Republic before going to Belgium for the last leg of the journey and then reaching the UK. Many make it – others don't. Some turn back when things go horribly wrong or they realise they have been tricked by traffickers. Nevertheless, the UK is favoured as the best destination because it is believed to be easier to go around undetected. There are no ID checks like in Europe. The fear of going to countries like the Netherlands is that they will end up in a refugee camp. In other European countries, police may stop them, arrest them, ask for ID and deport them if they don't have the correct papers.

# Placing the displaced

Young asylum seekers and refugees live across the UK, but the majority reside in the south east – London, Kent, Essex, Brighton and Hove and Bedfordshire. Smugglers are constantly on the lookout for weaknesses in coastal routes. There is a high number in Portsmouth because this is used as a route for smugglers. Many others 'arrive' in various other parts of the country, including Manchester, Liverpool and Birmingham, as a result of being smuggled into the country by lorry before being dropped off in various cities around the country. There are hardly any young asylum seekers in Cumbria or Cornwall, for obvious reasons. Placing young people in these exceptionally rural parts of the UK or areas without education provisions (such as ESOL programmes – English for Speakers of Other Languages), legal support or infrastructure, cultural diversity and/or little knowledge of how to support arrivals is pointless.

The placing of young people in the UK is still an ad hoc process that does not yield consistency or involve equal numbers being allocated to various areas and boroughs. The National Transfer Scheme (NTS) was launched in 2016 to encourage all local authorities to volunteer to support unaccompanied asylum-seeking children (UASC) so there is a more even distribution of caring responsibilities across the country. Under the scheme, a child arriving in one local authority area already under strain caring for UASC may be transferred to another council with capacity. NTS was a voluntary scheme and resulted in only a third of local authorities agreeing to take part, many of which applied self-imposed levies on the numbers they accepted. The scheme is generally regarded as unsuccessful.

# Location, advice and support

Young people should be part of mainstream society. They should not just be referred to as refugees nor be placed solely in refugee groups. They need to be included in local youth clubs and football teams alongside citizen children who respect their diversity. Professionals need to be aware that those with language barriers and learning needs must be included, and that despite such issues these young people are no different to others. Young people need to be given choices and options. Many will already have been half-migrants, having come to the UK from other countries (Switzerland, Sweden and Italy). It's no good expecting them to be grateful and thinking that what they are offered is good enough (examples of inadequate provisions are outlined throughout this book).

When it comes to choices, the message needs to be firm and stipulate that a young person without LTR status must still be respected and given as many options as every-body else. These young people deserve positivity and the chance to harvest their aspirations and hopes. They all deserve a decent life. They all come with baggage and, in addition to this, must navigate themselves through the ups and downs of life like every other teenager, while waiting for a decision on their asylum claim. Therefore, hard questions need to be asked about better education provisions and mental health services.

Education is often seen to be good enough, but it is not. There needs to be a greater emphasis from the beginning. Horror stories abound of children being placed in schools during the second term and expected to catch up with the rest of the class. This is very poorly thought out, as is any ESOL provision that is found to be lacking in good-quality teaching for those with low language skills. Is it any wonder there is dis-engagement? In addition, why isn't it standard to offer mental health provision to all of these young people, especially at the beginning? Everybody recognises that trauma 'is to be expected' in young asylum seekers. Therefore, CAMHS (the Child and Adolescent Mental Health Service) needs to address their support and be equipped to deliver a service to all young people (which is currently not the case – see Chapter 4 on trauma for further explanation).

Many professionals believe that the fundamentals are lacking for UASC and care leavers. There is never one assigned professional who oversees a young person's life journey from when they arrive as children to their transition into adulthood. It is considered that non-partisan options are rarely available, especially with the numerous workers and professionals young people experience when they leave and are replaced. A guardianship service was piloted in Scotland, where an independent advocate was assigned to be a stable contact in the young person's life for as long as they were needed. The Scottish Guardianship Service provided young people with a guardian and a friendly face who supported them through the daunting asylum process – a familiar face among the maze of lawyers, social workers and Home Office officials. The guardianship pilot was a success, with very positive feedback from the young people involved, and demonstrated that there is a real need for a permanent guardianship service to be established and rolled out across the whole of the country.

# Untapped potential

These are young people who can excel. Many have so much talent and want to learn. Some, through hard work and perseverance, do better than some citizen children. They respond to encouragement; however, this is not given by professionals as much as it should. Things could change in the blink of an eye if the system developed a better attitude, respect and quest to implement better human rights and laws. But, unfortunately, this is part of the toxic, hostile and dangerous world we live in and often boils down to humanitarian action. Every professional, whether they are at the front line or a policy maker, needs to question their own values and ask what is in their heart. They must question what they need to do to make the system fairer and better for every young person, and ensure that young people's humanitarian rights are met and protected. Instead of just talking about human rights they need to ensure they are implemented better. The Council of Europe has a strong trajectory and sharp focus towards humanitarian sponsorship and partnership from its member countries. However, the UK needs to listen to what it says or risk losing its humanitarian values. A prime example of this is its current practice of allowing more refugees to enter the UK under resettlement programmes and family reunification schemes, which are practically non-existent at present, bar a few cases.

Some young people lie about their LTR status because they fear their peers will judge them for not being as advanced as they are. However, for young asylum seekers and refugees, their peers are their main source of comfort, advice and affection, and are often their most trusted companions because they have all been through similar experiences. These young people may have fled their country of origin for the same reason or they might have been forced to flee from their own families because of planned honour killings, homophobia, forced marriages and/or retaliation. Professionals also need to learn more about the social lives and outside interactions of young people away from services. What happens when they fall out with their friends over money? How do they cope with the stress of language barriers and exam pressures? How do they cope with puberty, romance and how do they react to bodily and emotional changes? Do they do what most or all young people do? Professionals need to contrast and compare more, but little research in this area is yielding.

# Young female asylum seekers

Women comprise just over 5 per cent of young asylum seekers and refugees, and are either part of Syrian resettlement scheme families or come from Eritrea, Ethiopia and Vietnam. There are also some from Somalia who came with their families, as well as a small number of Albanians who entered as USAC. Vulnerability, exploitation and trust issues are commonplace among them all. These are young people who have been used and abused all their lives. Some of those from Somalia and Eritrea will have been subjected to female genital mutilation (FGM).

Many of the young women from African countries have worked as servants and several will have been sexually and physically abused. Others are taken to the UK as part of forced marriage, mainly from Afghanistan, on their husband's immigration pass and have often endured domestic violence. Others are often sold into modern-day slavery – after being promised in marriage at the age of 11 or 12. Most come from patriarchal societies and still bear the hallmarks of expecting to be told what to do by men.

Vietnamese girls from poor families are often trafficked to the UK. Parents sell their children under the agreement that the children have to work to repay the debt. The girls are often tattooed with designs of lips on their arms and hands – especially those who have been earmarked to work in the sex industry. Although carers are advised to refrain from allowing these young people access to mobile phones, they still manage to go missing because they are fearful of their families' safety back home – they know the hardship and suffering that their parents and families will endure if they don't fulfil their side of the bargain to the traffickers, who are renowned for being threatening and violent.

Professionals working with these young women mainly concentrate on helping them to determine the difference between positive and unhealthy relationships. They are offered explanations as to what is healthy and unhealthy because this needs to be clarified, along with what it means for somebody to be vulnerable and at risk of exploitation. These young women often thrive in education. Many attended schools back home and value education. They are also known to be compassionate, given their own personal suffering, and many seek training to become teachers or to work in the care system.

With regard to LTR status there is sometimes a debate in the Home Office between those who are Eritrean and those from Ethiopia. Some Eritreans live on the border and vice versa. Some were sold into wealthy households as young children and have grown up there. Their circumstances in these scenarios can therefore be ambiguous, but this is mainly so for young Eritrean women who find their backgrounds difficult to prove.

Naturally, those refused LTR status don't want to go back to their country of origin. They have nothing to return to – no families, no future and little hope. Only further hardship and suffering awaits them. They want to escape a life of servitude. Many of those who are refused status run away to London. Some seek solace in their Orthodox churches, which too can lead to problems because these churches are unregulated and often refuse to co-operate with the authorities. Although they may help these young females by offering them a place to stay, safeguarding is a prime concern.

# LGBT issues

Being gay carries great stigma in many Islamic and African countries. Most young refugees are not 'out' before arriving in the UK. A few are found out when somebody sees a picture on their phone that may reveal their sexual orientation, and/or some are caught in compromising situations with same-sex friends. These situations have led to family beatings and threats of forced marriages and honour killings unless such friendships are ended. Even the authorities get involved. They try to trick young people who use the gay dating app Grindr by initiating a meeting. When the young person arrives at their agreed rendezvous point, they are immediately arrested. It is not considered that some young people are bisexual or perhaps questioning their sexuality. There are others, young men for example, who are targeted because they present effeminately, and a few have even said they were blackmailed, resulting in them being forced into sexual activity with somebody before they fled their country.

In some countries, such as Iran, if somebody is found to be gay, they are threatened with forced gender reassignment surgeries. Some are even carried out just to avoid imprisonment. The point here is that young people who grow up in these countries become instinctively cautious of the hatred directed at the LGBT community. They have no experience of friendly or acceptable words for being gay that haven't been associated with images of something that is bad, wrong or evil. In general, the whole of society in these countries is deeply homophobic and reporting any hate crimes to the police is pointless, because many are corrupt and would escalate matters instead of offering a resolution. This makes it easier for some young people to be sexually abused and trafficked to the UK.

Life in the UK for young gay and lesbian asylum seekers and refugees is often not easy. Arriving here might bring freedom from the dangers back home, but they are sometimes replaced by new problems and threats. Isolation from their community is commonplace if their LGBT status becomes known, and therefore friendships are curtailed. There is also isolation from religious groups, for example, although there is one mosque in London that welcomes LGBT people. Orthodox and evangelical churches are not renowned for reaching out to the LGBT community, and gay conversion therapies are often suggested when the topic of someone being gay or lesbian transpires.

Few young people are aware of the organisations they can reach out to for help – although these are mainly based in London; however, telephone contact where emotional support is offered is more widely publicised. The point is that most of these young people need a lot of emotional support and counselling. The long-term effects of having to pretend to be somebody else takes its toll on young minds. Often these young LGBT asylum seekers require extensive interviewing. They find it particularly difficult to open up and talk freely about their feelings and experiences because it is not part of their cultural norms to be transparent.

Predators seek out young refugees with the intention of sexually exploiting them, and stories are recounted of some young people being offered money or drugs for sex. These are prime candidates for predators in the sense that they are good looking, vulnerable and naïve, with many coming from poor backgrounds and lacking in education. They are deficient in resilience, confidence and self-worth. They are not used to talking to people about sex and they know little about HIV or safe sex. When somebody approaches who appears caring and nurturing and promises to help, young people are susceptible of falling into a trap that leads to exploitation and dangerous encounters where drinks are spiked and followed by sexual abuse, including rape.

The Home Office requests that applicants for asylum evidence their sexuality. This is often not an easy thing to prove and it is particularly difficult for UASC. Some offer evidence of threats they have received from family members or show photos or other information from Facebook to support their application, but it's not easy. The Home Office, it is sometimes felt, is looking for clues that might disprove somebody belonging to the LGBT community – for example, if a boy likes football or if they listen to certain types of music or singers – but what this ultimately amounts to is negative stereotyping and veiled homophobia. A great worry hangs over young asylum seekers who are LGBT. They fear that not getting their LTR could lead to later incarceration in a detention centre with a strong male and macho presence, and where stories of sexual abuse and rape are not uncommon.

Despite the obstacles, there is still much fight for life in these young people who have come to the UK to escape persecution because of their sexuality. Often their country, family and communities have rejected them, but they still hold a place in their hearts for their country and culture despite it having turned its back on them. There is also a great capacity for hope in these young people, with stories from LGBT charities reporting that many eventually meet partners and find love and fulfilment in the process. This is sometimes with other asylum seekers and refugees, but also from mainstream society including British and other nationalities from around the world.

# Not one of us

Most asylum seekers and refugees come from countries where there are no equality laws. After getting refugee status or humanitarian protection, they cease being thought about as exiles, but also have little hope of ever being able to return to their country of origin. Others come to the UK and think it's a great place to be. There is a 'honeymoon' period where they feel safe and secure, but after this expires the harsh reality sets in when they realise that life here is tough for asylum seekers. Their mental health is affected and shattered because of difficulties integrating into British culture, accessing services and developing an identity. Their life chances are impaired if they don't get the correct support.

After arriving in the UK, young people still need to be protected from further traumas including sexual and financial trauma and other forms of exploitation and abuse. They also need to regain their health after poor nutrition and malnutrition, missed immunisations, and poor dental care. As you will read at various times throughout this book, Britain is better at looking after asylum seekers and refugees than some other European countries, but whether they are taken care of well enough, in line with our resources, is questionable. There is still poor consistency across the country in terms of provisions and services. Where somebody arrives often determines where they are placed. It is noted though that those arriving in multi-cultural areas do better and stand out less from other minorities.

Some asylum seekers and refugees feel they must justify their right to be in this country, which leads one to wonder if they begin to feel, as they get older, that they are not safe or secure. Do they feel the world is telling them they do not belong – although they may appear to live happy lives? This can result in feelings of rejection and all kinds of fears. It is also terribly unfair given that the British economy would not be as strong were it not for all the small businesses that were created by previous generations of refugees that now employ many young people in their barber shops, corner shops, restaurants and takeaways. Instead of being prejudicial, society needs to embrace difference and value and respect these services that many people take for granted.

For those whose asylum claim is waiting to be processed, the legality of being forbidden to work needs to be investigated because it is self-defeating for many of these people. The bar on doing voluntary work should also be investigated – the Home Office's presumption that young people could seek payment or part-payment, or believe that it could lead to employment, is unfair and not backed by evidence.

Discrimination is present amongst the police force, who should be better informed about young people in these situations. I was told a story about a boy who was picked up for riding a bicycle without lights and ended up spending the night in the police cells. The police were unable to quickly verify his identity or legal status. Asylum seekers, especially those who are black, are often viewed the same as migrants because some police officers are unable to differentiate between them. The police are also often suspicious of young people who work in fast food outlets. For example, if one person is of interest to them and they go to that person's workplace and see other young people, they will question them as well. This is unnecessary and unjust.

# Conclusion

It is not easy making sense of 'abandoned' lives, where young people strive to build a future for themselves in the absence of direct family support and parental guidance. And yet there are those in Britain who readily discriminate against young asylum seekers and refugees. Have we lost empathy in Britain? Is it not essential now, more than ever before, to live harmoniously in a society that welcomes others?

Many people voted in the 2016 Brexit referendum because of strong views over immigration and asylum seekers. There are those who feel Britain is too lenient and allows too many asylum seekers into the UK. The evidence though, as mentioned earlier, is the opposite. Britain has fewer asylum seekers and refugees than other main European countries. Blaming them for the economic problems in the UK is folly. They are not the problem, but it may take years before the finger of blame is pointed elsewhere.

The evidence instead argues towards these young people having good social conduct and social norms, along with strong values and work ethics. As a nation, we need to be curious because we can learn from each other in the most surprising of ways. We need to look at our own attitudes and try to be a little more generous. What if the situation was reversed, as it was during the two world wars when British children were sent to countries like the United States and Australia for safety?

# Chapter 2 | Social work practice

# Introduction

Social work practice does not involve greater variety – in terms of diversity, human difficulties and trauma – than for those working with young asylum seekers and refugees. The role of corporate parents is perhaps the most prevalent in this field of social work, given that most of these young people, particularly UASC, are living here without the direct support of their parents. This chapter looks primarily at the services offered to UASC by local authorities and social workers, and the challenges faced by both sides.

Somebody who is deemed UASC upon arrival in this country will remain under Children's Services until the age of 18 (even if they are only months away from their eighteenth birthday). They are then transferred to the leaving care team, where they are given a personal adviser until the age of 25. And yet it is noted that despite the support given by professionals to these young people, life in the UK is still difficult and challenging, whether or not they receive refugee status. The challenges facing social workers are often myriad and complex. It's a constant battle of identifying gaps between the social work agenda, which is directed by local authorities, and the global agenda of asylum, coupled with immigration policies and ensuring human rights are upheld.

# Safe authority

The principle of young person first and asylum seeker second needs to be a prime realisation, because this will bring greater understanding of those who have come to the UK having fled from something in order to seek a safer and better life. Over time, social workers get to know young people really well and, ultimately, it could be argued that it is not their responsibility to inform the Home Office if discrepancies are found in their stories. With the exception of reporting criminal behaviour, can social workers fulfil a trusting, caring and supportive role for young people if they report information from private discussions that contradicts what is already known about the young person's background? Can social workers be expected to be valued and respected for their expertise if young people are unable to trust them?

I have known social workers who have had doubts about young people's stories, including doubts that they were telling the truth about changing their religion or about not having close family members in the UK. The majority chose not to inform the Home Office because of insufficient proof. The main aspect of contention, though, is age disputes – which I will expand upon later in the book. It could be said that social workers, in the main, try their best to build trust with their young people and in return young people turn to them because they trust their advice and guidance. Social workers are a sort of 'professional friend' because they fulfil the role of corporate parent. It is essential for a good working relationship that there is honesty, trust and boundaries, but this does not exclude humour and good rapport. The more a social worker knows a young person and has a good relationship with them, the more the young person will listen and respect them. This is particularly useful in times when young people need to confront difficult situations or when they are struggling with their emotional health. It also helps when they need to be corrected for misdemeanours like smoking in their accommodation or having overnight guests when it's against the rules of their tenancy.

Another dimension, though, to this quandary is that social workers working with young asylum seekers and refugees can sometimes feel they operate in a world of secrets and lies. Coupled with this are the continuous demands they have to contend with, some of which are unrealistic, such as asking to be housed in different parts of the country because they believe it is their entitlement or requesting money for material goods when funding for such items is not available. When such requests are refused, it often leads to social workers feeling like ineffective providers. It is necessary to realise, however, that secrets and lies are part of the young person's sense of survival and that it takes time for them to trust their social workers before accepting them as a 'safe authority' in the sense that social workers are different from the police or immigration officials from the Home Office.

# Fragile lives

Little research is done on asylum-seeking children and their psychological development. There is a dearth of knowledge about the learning needs of young refugees, including learning difficulties and levels of autism – or disability in general. Research needs to be done with young people and not just be about them. Academics need to adapt their method to working directly with young people and with social workers for first-hand experiences.

Young asylum seekers and refugees have little option but to accept that endurance has always been part of the refugee experience, because nothing happens fast in the world of bureaucracy. Choices are limited. Understanding and empathy are sometimes in short supply. It is, therefore, little wonder that many of these young people feel like they live on the fringes of society as observers of the world, instead of being fully operational members, while they await their Home Office decision.

Life can appear unfair and fragile as they continue their day-to-day living, but at the same time they have to carry around with them a sense of a foreshortened future. How can a young person plan for the future when they don't know their long-term immigration status? How can social workers help young people create a home in the UK and learn to become ordinary citizens given this uncertainty? The answers are never simple. Very little is sometimes known about the lives of the young people before they arrived in the UK. More investment needs to be given to this, despite young people often being reluctant to divulge personal information. Some social workers will have sight of personal statements prepared by the young people with their solicitors, but others won't. Some social workers will complete genograms and timelines with their young people, but others won't. Some social workers carry out comprehensive Child and Families assessments with their young people, while others will complete only the bare minimum of information. The overall cost of this poor investment means that some young people end up getting an unsatisfactory service from Children's Services, along with an inability to develop a sense of belonging in an alien country and without their families.

## Lawi (17) from Iraq

*The problem with the Middle East is that there is a deep ideology about religion. It is about controlling people because they do everything the government tells them to do. The government do not like people to learn too much Arabic because they may start questioning things in the Qur'an, like I did – even though they only read the Qur'an and don't understand what they are reading. And these people do not read anything else, so they don't know anything about other ideas, religions or philosophy. I was very good at Arabic at school. I was also very good at asking questions as a child. I questioned why the Qur'an said if you are not Muslim it is okay for you to be attacked and killed. Shi'a and Sunni Muslims say this to each other all the time – one accuses the other of not being Muslim.*

*People ask questions about the Middle East and wonder why it has so many rich oil countries while so many people are poor, and why so many refugees come from these parts of the world. The answer is in the control of governments and Islam. I came from a religious family and they hated me questioning Islam and the prophet, Muhammad. Islam is the red line in Middle East countries, where people instinctively never question or challenge it. People are constantly told to be afraid of God and to be scared of hell. My father repeatedly slapped me when I asked a question that was considered disrespectful about Islam or the Prophet, but even from a young age this did not deter me from wanting more and more information, because so much of what I read in the Qur'an prompted me to ask the reasons why, especially when I came across things that did not make sense.*

*And then over a four-year period, I secretly read the Bible and the Torah and other books about religion and philosophy. During this period, I also stopped praying and doing Ramadan. I gathered all of my own information and, at the end of it, I made up my mind that I no longer wanted anything to do with Islam. I felt it in my heart and knew I was making the right decision to reject it. My uncle told me he would have me killed if I didn't start obeying my father, who locked me inside the house for a month after I told my family I no longer wanted to be Muslim. I believed my uncle about having me killed. His words echoed in my head when he repeatedly threatened me, saying things like, 'If you are going to be like this and you are not going to change and obey the rules of our religion, then I will kill you myself.'*

*Having somebody killed in Iraq is easy, and killing a Muslim who has rejected their religion is very forgivable in the eyes of the law. I know of people who murdered members of their family for various wrongdoings and ended up only serving six months in prison. Everybody has a gun in Iraq, so I would probably have been shot if I didn't manage to escape with the help of another close relative who heralded me to safety and eventually paid the money to get me out of the country.*

# Corporate parenting

Various levels of knowledge and expertise can be found in care teams that look after young asylum seekers and refugees. Social workers will be knowledgeable in social work systems and processes and what entitlements young people are eligible to, but may have insufficient understanding about the situational circumstances of these young people in general, barring scant pieces of information picked up on random training courses. This sometimes-dismal lack of knowledge can be found even among senior practitioners who operate in a robotic manner that underlies a cavalier attitude towards the young people, whether intentional or not.

The role of corporate parent is often misunderstood. I have often heard managers tell young asylum seekers that social workers are *'like your parents'* as if this was a good thing – and that social workers are capable of replacing their real parents. The main role is to ensure they have been provided with accommodation and services that will assist them to thrive. Kohli (2011, p 25) sums this up as follows.

*There is evidence to show that beyond the legal permission to continue to remain, asylum seeking children begin to feel safe in the day to day by finding predictable patterns, shapes and rhythms of living, by being in a good school, getting prompt medical care, and finding trustworthy, reliable and companionable people, adults and peers.*

However, the relationship between a social worker and young person is a totally professional one and, although there is a level of friendliness involved, its scope is never capable of taking over as the role of a parent on any level. Nevertheless, close bonds are formed and young people often remain in touch with their social workers after they progress from Children's Services to the 18plus aftercare service.

UASC are prepared for independent life through specific activities in reception care facilities. Here they are helped to increase their independence – cook their own meals, do their own shopping and laundry, etc. They attend ESOL classes and are given integration advice and guidance before moving into shared independent accommodation in the community. Only those under 16 or those considered particularly vulnerable are placed in foster care. Local authorities have contracts with housing providers who source mainly four-bedroomed properties to rent. UASC are given an Essential Living Allowance (ELA) – usually amounting to the equivalent given to those on income support – which is paid to them fortnightly. UASC are under Section 20 of the Children Act 1989 and therefore have a named social worker and once placed in the community they will get registered with a local GP, dentist and optician.

Looked After Child (LAC) reviews take place twice yearly with an Independent Reviewing Officer ensuring that a young person's needs are being met. Recommendations are made around education, health and independent living skills, for example, to ensure services are put into place to optimise opportunities for the young person to thrive. Young people are also eligible to request an advocate from a charity, where somebody will attend review meetings to ensure the young person's views are heard.

Each young person under the age of 16 is given a care plan. Once over the age of 16, this is transferred to a Pathway Plan. Both plans are similar, although a Pathway Plan for older young people is designed to navigate them towards independence and adulthood. This will include eight key components: living arrangements, daily living skills, identity, family and social networks, emotional well-being, education and employment, health, and finances. A social worker usually sees each young person at least monthly but, depending on their emotional needs and circumstances, contact may be more frequent. Other services given to young people include twice annual clothing allowances, gym memberships and laptop computers for college work.

In the lead up to young people preparing for their substantive interview with the Home Office, they see their immigration solicitors who are independent from the Home Office and Children's Services. They will help the young people prepare their personal statement for the Home Office, outlining why they are seeking protection in the UK. These statements are forwarded to the Home Office by the solicitor and will be used during an interview with the young person at a later date.

# Peer support

Time after time, I have seen young people take care of each other. Some of these will have come from cultures and families where it is the norm for older children to look after younger siblings. Eritreans, Sudanese and Ethiopians quickly come to mind as I have often seen supportive and caring relationships amongst these peer groups. Here are young people who previously developed nurturing skills in their families. This is indeed a protective factor and one that is humbling given the distant and aloof relationships that sometimes exist between young asylum seekers and professionals.

This peer support is particularly seen in social work teams where young people are placed in shared independent accommodation (irrespective of their ability to cope) and are often seen as de facto adults and not children. There are reasons for this. A prime example is the culture of disbelief that exists in the social work profession who believe some asylum seekers are older than they admit and sometimes over the age of 18, despite claiming to be younger. If the team is managed by somebody with prejudiced views towards young asylum seekers (this occurs more often than realised) and believes that many of the young people lie about their age, this hardening of practice is imparted to team members and leads to some social workers being unable to challenge this type of attitude. This results in young people receiving only minimal support upon the completion of a care needs assessment (ie money for accommodation and food only, which is the direct opposite to a holistic approach that would measure each young person's vulnerability and needs individually).

Even compassionate social workers in a generic Child in Need team can overlook young asylum seekers and refugees in their care because of heavy caseloads. If a young person is going to college, behaving well and keeping quiet, this can result in them being 'forgotten' about and taking second place to a citizen child who presents more vocally and problematic. These young people are simply left to look after themselves ineffectively and in circumstances that are not morally defendable. The end result is that there are many 16-year-old asylum seekers and refugees living in poor-quality shared accommodation who have inadequate coping mechanisms along with under-developed daily living skills.

# Standards of care

The standard of care varies enormously in different local authorities and this spreads out to foster carers, social workers and support workers. There is a mixture of good care as well as poor standards of care that are not widely recognised. Independent Foster Placements (IFA) are noticeably better than those offered by local author-ities, but cost more. A lack of financial incentives for local authority foster carers has lessened their numbers, resulting in more outsourcing to independent fostering agencies for placements. Sometimes, little or not enough emphasis is placed on cul-tural expectations, language, communication skills and empathy amongst foster carers who fail to understand that UASC sometimes feel awkward living with them and that they are often viewed as strangers by the young people.

An advocate told me how she once went to a LAC review where the young person didn't like the foster placement they had been allocated. The social worker couldn't understand why the young person felt that way – the house was nice and the foster carers were lovely people. So, she asked him to draw a picture of his ideal home. Everybody wondered what exactly was wrong. Was the house too big or too small? Did he not like his room? Or did he dislike the neighbourhood? To everybody's aston-ishment, the young person drew a picture of his mother, father and three brothers. There was nothing wrong with the foster carers or their house – what was missing was the young person's family.

IFA foster carers often undergo better training than local authority foster carers and generally have better understanding of the asylum system and the legal frame-work. This is certainly useful given that a lack of knowledge, coupled with little or no awareness of trauma training or the experiences endured by UASC before and during their journeys to the UK, often leads to placement breakdowns. Foster carers, in gen-eral, also have limited understanding of the cultural differences that young people experience once they arrive in the UK, where they are 'expected' to automatically settle without any difficulties. Instead, Children's Services and social workers often appear to complete assessments that fail to address these important factors.

The quality of shared independent accommodation is better in recent years than it used to be. In the past, it was not uncommon to find young asylum seekers and refugees living in squalid and totally unsatisfactory accommodation, with cockroaches and vermin. However, there are still huge gaps and differences in the resources provided by different local authorities. Some young people live in good-quality accommodation with adequate furnishings and modernised kitchens and bathrooms, while others live in rundown and sparsely furnished houses that don't have a television and generally don't radiate a welcoming feeling.

Some young people often don't have the life skills to live alone. The degree of responsibility is sometimes too much and it is hard for them to engender a sense of belonging under these circumstances. They often don't feel safe in these houses either, and are vulnerable to gangs, groups and dangerous individuals. If one person brings drugs into the house, the police target the house. This results in everybody who lives in the house having their name and swab taken, and the Home Office is informed – so even those young people living at the address who are totally innocent of any wrongdoing are caught up in this criminality. This is dreadfully unfair and unless a social worker or the young person's solicitor writes to the Home Office to clarify the situation, the issue can be negatively recorded against them.

Many young people in these placements form good friendships and create a 'family' of their own, while others prefer to live separate and individual lives. Ideally, it is preferable when a household of young people get on well together and form close bonds, although not every professional will agree with this. A female worker from an advocacy group told me a story of how one day she went to a review meeting at a house with four young males. She arrived early, before any other professionals, and immediately upon entering was greeted by a lovely smell of food in the kitchen where the boys had cooked a meal together. Shortly afterwards, the social worker arrived and rather shockingly started shouting at the young people, telling the boys that they should all cook separately for themselves because they all needed to learn how to live independently.

There are other examples of poor practice, with stories told of workers failing to address young people properly by their names, and some young people being liked more by workers than others and therefore receiving preferential treatment, as well as extra birthday or Christmas gifts. Then there were issues of some social workers making false promises that they were slow to fulfil. Does it take months to get a young person a copy of the Qur'an or a Tigrigna Bible? Is it really necessary to quibble over the payment of a £5 phone card for a young person to call their family in Eritrea? With regard to other poor standards of care, examples included care providers requesting delegated authority from social workers and waiting months to receive it, and requests for risk assessments about those at risk of exploitation that were often delayed and took an inordinate amount of time to be produced.

## Lawi's stance on social workers

*Social workers carry out the work that the government expects them to do. They help with housing, education and health because that is what the government has asked, but they don't care about us. They don't know what young people have gone through. My social worker is not very good. He doesn't come to see me often. I ring him, but he never answers. He never does anything for me. I really don't think he cares. To me, a good social worker is somebody who reacts quickly when you tell them you have a problem. This makes someone feel they are worth the trouble. It shows they care and it shows that they value how you can impact on this country.*

*When I had my interview with the Home Office, my social worker didn't attend. Instead, he sent a social work assistant. She told me that this was the first time she had ever attended one of these interviews. This, to me, is an example of how he doesn't care for me. Doesn't care if I stay or have to leave. Doesn't care what sort of life I've had before I came here, or what sort of life I'll have after I'm 18.*

*Young people need social workers who will push them in the right direction. Some young people don't care about education or jobs. They just want to be free. But you need a social worker who cares about your education, because when you are 16 or 17 you don't think about these things. Some young people just speak street language (I'm cushty, mate!) and don't care about speaking English properly or being able to read or write. For others, it's about going to college just to keep your attendance up. I know some who do this, but even after a year at college they can still only speak a few words of English. They don't make enough effort to learn. Young people need social workers who will help them see their futures and what this is going to be like. They need to be told what they need to do if they want to get a good job.*

# Sub-groups

While young people can have a propensity to complain about their social workers and the services they receive, it is useful to look at research that indicates that adult asylum seekers can be placed into various categories including different personalities, neediness and assertiveness. Hulewat (1996) outlined three sub-groups in asylum seekers and refugees but many professionals feel these traits equally apply to young asylum seekers.

1. Help me get started.

2. Take care of me.

3. You must do things my way.

I wish to expand further on these three groups and describe the different types of personality behind each group. It might be able to explain if there is an innate need of survival that comes to the surface when young people are placed in unfamiliar situations that is coupled with fear and uncertainty.

*Help me get started*
*These young people are strong-willed, focused and determined to succeed. They are polite and respectful and willing to work with professionals in order to achieve their goals. They have a strong desire to do well in life.*

*Take care of me*
*These young people often present as helpless and lackadaisical. They are often resistant of independence or want independence on their terms. They are often attention seeking and ask for help with the simplest of things.*

*You must do things my way*
*These young people are often domineering, challenging and demanding, with unrealistic expectations. They are selfish and put themselves first over others. They dislike authority and are prone to failure because of their stubbornness.*

Consider these sub-groups as children being looked after under Section 20 in terms of help by local authorities in key areas: financial assistance for food and toiletries, housing, clothing, education and health needs, including psychological help. In doing so this will assist in understanding the different expectations and demands presented by young people who come with different types of emotional intelligence and abilities to cope in their new circumstances. We need to see the children themselves as ordinary citizens – wanting ordinary lives despite the extraordinary circumstances that have propelled them many thousands of miles away from their country of origin and their families. They deserve no less but, unfortunately, they often encounter prejudice and discrimination from the very system that should be protecting them.

# Empathy and compassion

My own personal background is very different to most indigenous social workers. I grew up on a farm in the west of Ireland and arrived in the UK in my early twenties, before going to university as a mature student. I never saw a black person before

I was 16. I was ignorant about different cultures and diversity issues, owing to my rural upbringing. I never set foot on a council estate before I became a social worker. Although I never went through any of the horrific experiences that many asylum-seeking children endure, I grew up in Ireland during the height of the Northern Ireland conflict.

When I first came to the UK in the late 1980s, I experienced discrimination because of the IRA and the violence and brutality this represented. So I understand what it feels like to be made feel unwelcome, to be an outsider, although I would never compare this to a young asylum seeker coming to the UK, thousands of miles away from home. After all, asylum seekers are people who flee their home country, often due to major conflicts or because of serious human right abuses, and who seek refuge in another country by lodging an asylum application. These young people endure severely interrupted childhoods and separation. It is necessary to step back and empathise with what it feels like to be in their shoes. Is it comparable to feeling the stress, trauma and guilt some children experience when their parents separate and divorce, or is it several times worse? I can't help but wonder if it is also coupled with a longing for everything to go back to the way it was before they left, but knowing that this will never happen.

Have social workers failed in their duty of care? It is not uncommon for some social workers to feel that young asylum seekers and refugees should be grateful for the help they are given. One advocacy worker told me how appalling it was to hear a social worker tell a young person that they cost the local authority £40,000 a year. Of course, this is just one example of a young person placed in foster care (a child living in shared independent accommodation costs less than £10,000 a year). The point here is that social workers need to remember that UASC have had interrupted childhoods. They have all lost something and experience constraints and pressures. Are they really abusing the system? Would any of us do things differently if we were in their shoes? Some might say that the UK has a debt to pay to several countries that UASC come from – for example, Iraq – and that the UK ought to feel obliged to correct this wrongdoing.

It is essential to see the potential of these young people and for their contribution to the UK after living here for a few years to be recognised, in the sense they become integrated, law-abiding citizens who are either attending college or are in employ-ment. Yet, local authorities receive criticism from voluntary organisations who feel that some social workers lack compassion. Comments made to me during my research included how some social workers devote insufficient time to attend legal meetings and hear statements being prepared or fail to request a copy of the young person's statement, resulting in these organisations remaining unaware of the young person's background story and the difficulties they encountered before and during their journey. They won't hear stories of the emotional wrench these young people have faced when leaving their parents behind. Neither will they be fully briefed about the young person's emotional scars stemming from their background.

Furthermore, advocacy groups are fearful that the main reason there is sometimes a lack of empathy in some local authorities towards UASC is because of cost-cutting exercises and the saving of resources. Charities are sometimes over-relied upon by local authorities who try to exonerate themselves from helping young people from their own resources – an example might be sending somebody to a food bank rather than giving them money or buying them food. This raises the question of whether local authorities are inadvertently creating the next generation of the underclass. Expecting these young people to live on bare essentials is hardly congruent with raising a generation of nurtured and valued young people.

The life of a young asylum seeker disintegrates if they are declined refugee status, which often leads to withdrawal of support from local authorities (more about this in Chapter 5), but the pitfalls of such cost saving often leads to lifestyles of drugs and criminality – or young people end up 'vanishing' and go underground without trace. This is particularly relevant to those who reach – or are reaching – the point of Appeal Rights Exhausted (ARE) in their asylum application, and especially those who do not sign a Home Office agreement for Section 4 funding until their deportation date is agreed (those who sign will be expected to live in cramped living conditions and be given £30 a week for food).

There is an enormous human cost to all of this, which is unnecessary and can be avoided. Can you imagine if research was carried out on this cohort of young people that highlighted how much misery is caused to people's emotional health, or the financial cost involved in repairing the damage to these young people, along with prison costs for those who enter the criminal justice system – and how much it costs to keep young people incarcerated in deportation centres for infinite periods of time?

# Training for social workers

Training for social workers is crucial in all areas of the asylum process but at the moment very few are specifically trained in this area – or attend training that would assist them in not making errors of judgement that result in profound effects on young people's lives. Throughout this book, I will cite examples of this. During my research, I met with the charity *Safe Passage* where I was told how mesmerised they sometimes were with the mistakes and injustices that have taken place as a result of botched social work practice. Some examples were given of how previous resettlement schemes (eg Dubs Agreement) have experienced horror stories of young people getting aged assessed even though they were given five years' LTR status upon arrival as part of a government-endorsed resettlement programme. This was done with the consent of the local authority. It was found that there was a total lack of understanding of the difference between spontaneous arrivals and those coming under resettlement schemes – mainly Syrian refugees. Further details of this will be expanded upon in later chapters.

I was also told by Safe Passage that it was also felt that a much better understanding was needed of the Dublin Agreement and the assessment framework that needs to be carried out with family members in the UK who are willing to sponsor a child relative currently living in an EU country. For example, if the accommodation is not deemed suitable, it is the responsibility of the local authority to work with the council to ensure that suitable housing is found, rather than closing a referral at the first hurdle. The best interests of the child must be upheld and further options need to be explored to rectify the situation, because not doing so means that family members cannot be reunited. This will also be expanded upon further later in the book.

# Exploitation

In social work circles, it is thought there are fewer cases of child sexual exploitation (CSE) involving UASC than citizen children, although there is no statistical evidence to prove this.

The official definition of CSE, issued by the Department for Education (2017, p 5), is as follows.

*Child sexual exploitation is not defined in law. Child sexual exploitation is a form of child sexual abuse. It occurs where an individual or group takes advantage of an imbalance of power to coerce, manipulate or deceive a child or young person under the age of 18 into sexual activity in exchange for something the victim needs or wants, and/or for the financial advantage or increased status of the perpetrator or facilitator. The victim may have been sexually exploited even if the sexual activity appears consensual.*

However, it is known that a high percentage of young people are frequently sexually abused during their journey to the UK. It is also known that a significant amount of sexual abuse took place in the 'Jungle' (*Calais Jungle* was a refugee and migrant encampment in the vicinity of Calais, France, which existed from January 2015, to October 2016).

In African countries, it is also known that children are trafficked and pass through Libya where they are kept in large warehouses. If they misbehave, they are taken out and physically beaten – some are raped to be taught a lesson. Professionals are also aware that UASC have experienced sexual abuse in their home countries, often within their families, before coming to the UK. This is noticeably prevalent in countries like Afghanistan.

Although there isn't any statistical evidence to suggest higher levels of CSE among UASC, predators are around – those who actively seek out children and young people or those who are opportunistic in their ploys when they encounter a vulnerable young person. Young people have been known to tell their social workers about strangers inviting them back to their homes or being promised gifts of iPhones or trainers for no apparent reason. Exploitation in general, though, is more commonly seen in young people drawn into 'county lines' (drug runners) and is particularly common in those who are NEET (Not in Education, Employment or Training). Young people whose asylum application is under appeal or those who have reached ARE and are coping badly with the uncertainty that hangs over them are susceptible to this, particularly if they have a poor relationship with their social worker or personal adviser and feel unsupported and undervalued.

The trafficking of children entering the UK is fairly common. The legal definition of 'human trafficking' under the Modern Slavery Act 2015 is as follows.

*A person commits an offence if they arrange or facilitate the travel of another person with the view to that person being exploited. A person can arrange or facilitate travel by recruiting, transporting, transferring, harbouring or receiving the victim, or by transferring or exchanging control over them. This includes internal trafficking, such as transporting or transferring victims by car, taxis, or public transport to towns across the country.*

Sometimes children as young as six or seven get smuggled into the UK in suitcases. Injuries include swollen necks, bruises, aching bones. Young people have also mentioned claustrophobia and being scared of the dark. There are also incidents of children who are unable to eat because they were so frightened. As mentioned in the previous chapter, trafficked children usually come from Albania, Vietnam, Nigeria and Eritrea. Vietnamese children are sometimes sold by their parents who are poor and living in poverty. These children are instructed by their traffickers as to when and where to run to in the UK if they fail to enter the country undetected. This usually occurs within 72 hours of arriving and while traffickers will not know addresses of where the children are placed in foster care, they are aware of the location of reception centres. They have been known to either turn up there or be in the vicinity awaiting opportunities to take the young person away to organised unidentified cannabis farms, where they are exploited as modern-day slaves for indefinite periods of time.

The trafficking of children and young people into the UK is constant. There is a whole group of children hidden in the UK who we know nothing about – they are on nobody's records. Thousands of children are unaccounted for and while some are picked up inadvertently by Children's Services, many are not. Some of these young people are from Afghanistan, who endure both labour and sexual exploitation. The latter is hard to identify because young people are reluctant and ashamed to divulge information. Many are brought to the UK, tempted with the prospect of a better life. They think they will be able to work and send back money to their families, but their aspirations are often squashed by the harsh reality of their exploitation that sees them living in squalid conditions with little money or food.

Trafficked children also come from Vietnam. These were boys initially, but now girls are also coming and they, too, are being used in the cannabis cultivation industry. Both Vietnamese boys and girls are also often sexually exploited. Young people are also trafficked from Albania as drug runners, and young Albanian boys in particular are victims of child sex abuse and exploitation. Then there are stories of young Eritreans who flee military service and end up being kidnapped and held in Libya until their families back home pay the ransom. Stories of families having to sell their homes to raise the money are not uncommon.

Foster carers should be better trained in trafficking. Some children go missing for a few hours or overnight, but are still under the influence of their traffickers who continue to abuse and exploit them before allowing them to return to their accommodation. These traffickers abuse the care system in the sense that they continue to exploit the young people without having to care, house or feed them. They know these vulnerable young people can be called upon and will do what they are told to because they are fearful of any reprisals – whether real or unfounded – for their families back home.

Safety plans are sometimes put into place when there is knowledge of exploitation or potential exploitation. In this instance, young people are not allowed to have their own mobile phones, they have restricted access to social media and their money is also monitored. They may also be placed under curfew and have to be home each evening by a certain time. Admittedly, young people have gone through some horrific journeys to reach the UK, so they are therefore amazed when these restrictions are placed upon them because it hinders their day-to-day activities. However, professionals working with these young people need to ensure that safety plans are explained properly to ensure they are seen as something good and designed to keep them safe, rather than being a punishment for something they haven't done.

Professionals who suspect that someone has been trafficked can make a referral to the National Referral Mechanism (NRM) at the Home Office, for young people suspected of being potential victims of trafficking and modern slavery, with the intention of getting them identified. While there might be good intentions behind this, it won't have any positive impact on the child's life other than further delaying their asylum application and placing them in limbo. There is still a lot of confusion around making these referrals, with many believing they are not in the best interests of the child. Some feel better training is required that answers how beneficial it is for the young person. UASC who are trafficked into the UK will have their asylum claim treated differently by the Home Office and it won't be concluded until a 'trafficking' decision is made, which can take years. This causes massive delays, looking for evidence that doesn't exist or can never be proven. Professionals question what difference it makes whether a child is smuggled or trafficked into the UK, since they will be safely taken care of by local authorities under Section 20. Because then, irrespective of their circumstances or background story, they will no longer be in a position to be exploited any further.

# Conclusion

Social workers enter these young people's lives usually during late adolescence. This is often without knowing much information about the young person's past. It would be useful to know more about their childhoods and adverse experiences, family life, schooling, friends, hobbies and interests, food, culture and religion – basically, everything they have left behind. There are two ways that better information gathering could be done than at present. First, through greater co-operation and liaison with solicitors and social workers, and with young people signing consent for their Home Office statements to be shared – which includes information about their background, trauma and reasons for claiming asylum. Second, obtaining better background information about the young person's childhood through a structured assessment specifically designed for asylum seekers. At present, local authorities do not have such an assessment tool and instead use the one designed for citizen children. In the absence of even a little background information, the social worker and young person become embroiled in sorting out the here and now, whether this is accommodation, college placement or dealing with their asylum claim. Often, it feels that whatever occurred before their arrival in the UK no longer holds any importance.

# Introduction

This chapter looks at how young people coming to the UK rebuild their lives. After recovering from their arduous journeys, they often face the future alone and find it difficult to navigate through an unfamiliar system or are surrounded by people they find hard to trust. The chapter also explores ways in which young people can succeed, although perseverance is often key to this.

Is Britain a good place for young asylum seekers and refugees to live? As a country, it receives fewer asylum applications relative to its population than most other European countries. Professionals claim that the government has failed to do enough to provide safe routes to Britain for refugees (the UK should have a moral duty to provide safe harbour) in line with its moral obligations as one of the richest countries in the world. The government has also imposed rules on family reunion for refugees in the UK that are considered inhumanely restrictive, because unaccompanied young refugees are not even allowed to sponsor their parents to come to the UK. Once here, young people often face poor housing, depression and post-traumatic stress disorder (PTSD), social isolation because of a lack of spoken English, loneliness, discrimination and racism. It sometimes appears that many odds are stacked against them from the outset, resulting in the survival of the fittest – but the moral question is why are things this way?

# Services

Services are inconsistent. And good services are dependent upon where the young person is placed. Where somebody lives is often a determining factor in creating stability. More often than not, accommodation issues among young asylum seekers and refugees are a bone of contention. The main reasons for dissatisfaction are personal tastes, poor-quality accommodation or being placed in an area they dislike – all of which leads to unhappiness.

Asylum-seeking children in the UK are not seen as a priority. Some local authorities even see them as a burden, problematic. The system has become corrupted because the human rights of children are not fully adhered to due to discrimination within local authorities and coupled with budgetary restraints. There are continuous signs of inequality and when implemented over a period of time this inequality becomes accepted. This has undermined the reputation of Children's Services as safeguarding vanguards. This discrimination sometimes starts with the director of services and then infiltrates itself down to managers and some social workers. These UASC are simply not seen as valued young people. Sadly, for some authorities, this has become the norm. On the one hand, on paper, we have a wonderful system for children in the UK. We have invested heavily in the Children Act, safeguarding, laws and the legal system and multi-agency partnerships, but most of this is not working – not implemented when it comes to these children. A quick examination of the system will show insufficient investment and that many of these young people are vulnerable and not valued. They are often seen as something the UK has to contend with, in order to camouflage their lack of care.

Services for young asylum seekers and refugees in the UK are good for those aged between 16 and 18 years. Their acute needs are met, but look at what happens after 18. The leaving care system is inadequate and more discrimination is visible here. When leaving care, UASC are seen differently – seen as 'foreign' – and until we recognise and change this, it will continue. We have to treat all children leaving care the same. Many of these young people do not have immigration determination – or some have failed claims and are at risk of no longer being in the leaving care system. They become *failed asylum-seeking young adults*. All of the work put into planning for their long-term outcomes is undermined. A portion of those referred to the National Asylum Support Service (NASS) will be detained and removed.

# Redefining Section 20

Some professionals feel that a much clearer definition is needed of what it means to be a child under Section 20 of the Children Act 1989. This was an interim solution for local authorities and was never designed for long-term usage for young people who came to the UK seeking asylum and who did not have their parents' agreement. The simple fact is there is no parental consent to Section 20, which defies its purpose. Some parents are dead – some are missing – and there is little or no chance of family reunification. Surely, this points in favour of the need for all UASC to be placed on Full Care Orders?

The main provision given to young people under Section 20 is accommodation. The type of accommodation is based on age, vulnerability and availability. Local authorities receive funding from the Home Office to cover the costs for accommodation, social work intervention and administrative support for each young asylum seeker and refugee in its care. Funding from the Home Office to local authorities comprises

£119 a day, which is about 50 per cent of how much it costs to keep the child in care. The Home Office funding stops if the young person is refused asylum, but restarts if they win their appeal. Funding is also provided from the Home Office to cover leaving care support, although the funding for over 18s is significantly less.

Accommodation provision by local authorities is contentious. Budgets are often blamed but there is also an unwillingness to spend large amounts of money on young asylum seekers. In the long term, this frugality is detrimental to young people both in terms of their mental well-being and their ability to make progress in their lives. Groark et al (2011, p 73) state:

*A secure base which promotes resilience and coping ability has been found to be of vital import-ance for young people to begin to make the transition to living a new and successful life in the UK. Focusing on the tangible conditions in which these young people can re-create a 'secure base' can help to reduce inequality and promote healing and recovery needed for them to overcome past trauma and current obstacles.*

Young people in larger cities have been known to be placed in areas where there is gang violence and in houses that are damp and in poor maintenance. They are invari-ably placed in accommodation where the rent is cheap and mainly in working-class neighbourhoods. The following is a list of the main types of accommodation that young people can find themselves placed in depending on age, vulnerability and capacity.

## Foster care

If a young person (UASC) comes to the UK aged 15, they will be placed in foster care – either with the local authority or, depending on availability, with a foster family through an independent fostering agency. Here they can live quite comfortably until they reach their eighteenth birthday, when they will be re-housed in shared inde-pendent accommodation and transferred to the 18plus leaving care team. The advan-tage of being in foster care means the young person will receive a lump sum from savings accumulated by foster carers throughout the time spent with them. This usu-ally amounts to a few thousand pounds.

Young people transferring from foster care to independent living (providing they have LTR status) will have to apply for Universal Credit. If they don't have refugee status, the local authority will pay them an Essential Living Allowance (money for food and basic essentials) until they receive their refugee status. There are currently very few Muslim foster carers in the UK, which is problematic given the high number of young people who are Muslims.

## Supported accommodation

Supported accommodation is run by various care companies who provide support staff on-site on a 24-hour basis. Young people have their own bedroom with shared facilities. Staff members have experience in helping young people develop independent skills, including shopping, budgeting, cooking and self-care. This type of accommodation is often a bridging gap for those leaving foster care and who are not yet ready to live in shared independent accommodation. Some young people will be placed in semi-independent accommodation with staff to help them develop skills towards independency if they lack skills or have a recognised vulnerability. However, these young people are in the minority and, for cost-saving purposes, the trend is primarily aimed at enabling them to live independently in shared houses as quickly as possible.

## Shared independent accommodation

This type of accommodation usually comprises four-bedroomed houses where young people have their own bedroom but share all other facilities. They live completely independently without any staff support and are expected to shop, cook and budget effectively by themselves without support. For those in semi-independent accommodation, they usually move out into shared independent accommodation once they reach 18 – unless circumstances dictate otherwise, for example, the young person has a mental illness. For those already in independent accommodation, they largely remain living in the same house but experience the transfer of their care from Children's Services to the 18plus leaving care team. They will also transfer to Universal Credit from the Essential Living Allowance. Unless they have previously been in foster care, they will not receive any financial pay-out given to them from savings accumulated during their time in foster care up until their eighteenth birthday.

## Supported lodgings

This is a form of temporary supported accommodation, with support provided by a host who is a private individual (or individuals) accommodating a young person in their home. This service provides accommodation and support for young people so they can live within a family-type environment while acquiring the skills and emotional resilience necessary to live independently from care.

## Staying put

This refers to situations in which a care leaver continues to live with their foster carer after their eighteenth birthday. They are usually supported by the local authority to remain in the placement until they are ready or they turn 21 (or up until the age of 25 if they are in higher education).

## Home Office accommodation

This is by far the harshest of all categories and applies to anybody over the age of 18 who is not a care leaver – or those over 18 who were care leavers but have had negative Human Rights Assessments (HRA) resulted in this provision being withdrawn – or to young people who have had negative age dispute assessments and have been deemed to be an adult. Often, these young adults are housed in terrible accommodation, riddled with damp and vermin, and operated by outsourcing giants such as Serco and G4S. They are isolated from any support services and denied English language lessons that would help them to integrate.

Examples of young adults living in these conditions mainly show that Britain's asylum system is nothing short of disgraceful in the way it imposes this level of destitution on able-bodied people who could contribute greatly to the country and the economy if given the chance. Asylum claims can take several years to process and a quarter of decisions are overturned on appeal. But while their claims are under consideration, asylum seekers are not allowed to work and pay taxes, and they are forced to subsist on an allowance of less than £5.50 a day. Years of living in these conditions can profoundly affect the physical and mental health of young adults who have already suffered significant trauma.

# The first two years

The first two years are crucial in the lives of asylum-seeking young people coming to the UK. They have to acclimatise to a new country, learn English and get used to new norms and cultures that are different to the ones they grew up with. Life can be split into two parts, with the young person either focusing their time on the past or on the present. Sometimes young people are more prone to looking at their losses rather than their gains, because insufficient life experiences don't enable them to put things into the correct perspective. There are often moments of resentment and anger when faced with hostility and discrimination. When faced with tension, homesickness is often felt. There are also moments of surprise and appreciation that the services in the UK are better than what is available in their countries of origin. But even when services surpass their expectations, they never compensate for being away from their families, familiar surroundings and culture. In psychological terms, it sometimes appears that the branches of the tree are here but the roots lie elsewhere.

Communication difficulties are commonplace for young people. They often complain about receiving letters and not understanding them because they are written in English, rather than their own language – although illiteracy in their native languages is also very high. This causes anxiety and frustration at not being able to reach social workers on the telephone. This impatience is the result of wanting instant assistance. There are two types of personality amongst young asylum seekers and refugees – those who are accepting of their circumstances and those who challenge professionals (often through rudeness and demands) because they believe they have a responsibility to take care of them. This is sometimes prompted after they have taken advice, often invariably wrong, from older adults in their respective communities. There are some young people who struggle with authority and this must be put in context with their background story, which may include being brutalised or abused by authoritative figures in their homelands. Social workers need to be calm and lead by example, through understanding, patience and being able to challenge appropriately in a manner that doesn't lead to undue confrontation or hostility.

Another hurdle that some young experience is the uprooting scenario. This occurs when young people who are in foster care in London are sometimes brought back to home boroughs when they reach 18. These are young people who were originally placed in London owing to a shortage of foster carers in their home borough when they first arrived in the country. Here are young people who have gone to school in London, made friends, become totally familiar with their local neighbourhoods and put down roots. Many will have received their LTR status. Expecting young people in this situation to uproot and move to an area where they have no connections is very poorly thought out – with the overarching reason being the cost implications of having to find them accommodation in London, which will be three times higher than in other parts of the country. This sudden shifting around causes terrible upheaval for the young person, who is expected to move to a new area away from school, college, friends and familiar networks. This transfer also impacts greatly on their chances of being placed on the housing register for social housing. Unfortunately, there is often a poor knowledge of council housing by social workers and 18plus about the rights of young people and therefore this is often brushed to one side if a local authority refuses to fund a London placement for a young person who has lived in a London foster placement but has now reached 18.

# Education

A great many young people will never have attended any formal type of education in their homelands before coming to the UK, particularly those from Afghanistan, Syria and Iran. Throughout their lives, they will have received little encouragement to learn or develop academic skills, including literacy. Their capability, application and intelligence are often not explored and merely left to chance. Going to school or an educational provision for the first time is often a shock, and for those with limited English it can entail stress and anxiety.

Examples of discrimination among various educational provisions are also commonplace. Some schools refuse to take or will try their hardest not to accept UASC because they fear they will impact on the school's reputation and their Ofsted standing because of poor exam results. There are also stories of some children who get stuck at the back of the class because teachers want them out of the way. Instances of nonsensical decisions get recounted among professionals. For example, it is known for UASC young people who were hardly able to speak any English and who have had no previous schooling to be expected to sit GCSE examinations. Overall, there appears to be no proper Year 11 academic package that is tailored to UASC who enter education for the first time during this period.

Rather than concentrating on helping them learn English and Maths (which is also a struggle for many of them), a lot of time is wasted on satisfying bureaucratic procedures. It is also considered unlucky for those children who arrive in the middle of the academic year, because they will often be unable to access education until the start of the next academic year. There are notably fewer resources among local authorities in providing home tutoring or private ESOL provisions to fill this interim period.

## Learning needs

The learning needs of young people with limited English are difficult to assess and result in missed opportunities that could highlight areas of vulnerability, particularly for those with learning difficulties. Additional support needs are often hidden by language, particularly mild learning difficulties that do not get spotted until young people start attending school or college. Often, this is too late and does not result in any meaningful support being put in place to assist in learning and academic development. Only a few UASC who attend secondary schools are assessed for an Education, Health and Care Plan (ECHP), which outlines a young person's special educational needs with recommendations of the help needed and how best a young person can be supported to achieve their potential in life.

Overall, this is a key area that needs further exploration because, currently, there isn't enough recognition or support in place for UASC with learning difficulties including dyslexia and dyspraxia – as well as the possibility of a small number having more entrenched psychiatric disorders, including Attention Deficit Hyperactivity Disorder (ADHD), Conduct Disorder and Oppositional Defiance Disorder (ODD). However, the possibility of these conditions existing in young asylum seekers and refugees is under-researched and often ignored. Instead, the young people are expected to attend educational establishments and learn with little assistance given.

## ESOL

This is the most common course for UASC after arriving in the UK and, in highly populated areas, further education colleges offer ESOL courses to meet demand. ESOL is a structured programme designed to help non-natives learn to speak English. It helps young people with essential language skills and is known for improving spoken English and helping to develop reading and writing skills. Most providers for UASC only teach up to Entry Level 3, which results in a high intermediate level of English, including reading and writing. Yet ESOL goes up to Level 5 and results in students being fully proficient in English, especially in literacy skills. It is noted, however, that there is a lack of pre-ESOL courses in the UK, designed for those only able to speak a little English or none at all.

ESOL provisions are difficult to find for those who want to enrol after the September and February intakes. Coupled with a shortage of tutors who can provide one-to-one home tuition or other courses to fill the vacuum that exists before the start of the next academic year, this means that many young people miss out.

Students who complete Entry Level 3 ESOL, and have developed sufficient literacy skills, can progress onto mainstream courses. Many choose practical vocational courses, like plumbing, engineering and carpentry. A few are successful enough to go to university.

## Employment

UASC are always worried about their legal status and it is often difficult to engage them in education, training and employment while they are waiting for their LTR. Many struggle with literacy and withdraw from ESOL courses, especially those who get their LTR and are eager to earn money. There are patchy provisions for providing services for job skills and preparing for interviews, and few services that offer mentors or guardians, because there is a constant battle for funding.

Often, social workers are expected to assist young people find employment. The result of poor literacy skills, though, ends in them securing only low-skilled, minimum wage jobs. Several find employment in barber shops, fast food restaurants or as delivery drivers for pizza companies. A small number become taxi drivers. As you will see later in this chapter, Universal Credit claims are unbelievably difficult to process and have become a deterrent for many young people to declare their earnings. This has opened a plethora of opportunities for exploitative employers to seize upon the vulnerabilities of UASC and has resulted in increased cash-in-hand payments, thus avoiding tax and National Insurance contributions.

# Family Tracing Service

Some young asylum seekers know the whereabouts of their families and are in a position to have regular telephone contact with them. Many others are not so fortunate – they have either been separated from their parents and siblings during the journey to the UK or their families that remained in their country of origin have since had to flee their homes and communities because of war, violence or threats of harm. The British Red Cross Family Tracing Service is totally confidential and impartial – unless safeguarding issues arise whereby it becomes a statutory duty to inform the young person's social worker. Several conversations and in-depth interviews and information gathering are undertaken with the young person when trying to trace his/her family. Any information gathered is then passed to the family tracing team in London, where it is processed and passed to the international office in Geneva before being circulated to various countries in the hope that the service will unite unaccompanied children and young people with their parents and families. Although it is a reputable service, the chance of finding the families of separated children is low and it is estimated to have an approximate 5 per cent success rate. There is also a level of scepticism among professionals who believe that young people use the family tracing service as a smokescreen – pretending they don't know the whereabouts of their families and not divulging information about family members already in the UK, using the service as a pretence to later tell the Home Office that they have done all they can to find their families but to no avail.

# Youth clubs and socialisation

In larger UK towns and cities, there are youth clubs that have groups for young asylum seekers and refugees, with such venues often playing host to young people from a plethora of different countries, languages, cultures and religions. These are great places for young people to make new friendships, meet others from their own communities and feel less isolated, and for those new to the country to find out more information about the local area. Activities can range from having a sports night to playing football, cricket and volleyball. Opportunities for swimming lessons are also given because it is found many young people don't know how to swim. English (ESOL) classes are also sometimes on offer.

Youth clubs are also ideal places for young people to offload their worries and concerns, and it is often here that staff members are informed of safeguarding issues. It is not uncommon for young people to complain about foster carers who lock them out of the house if they are not home at a certain time, or lock the kitchen overnight or refuse them food if somebody is late for a meal. Others have told of being asked to eat meals in their bedroom, separate from the foster carer's family. While enduring these circumstances, few people will be aware that the young person is also coping with something else that is going on back home – the death of a family member or the discovery that someone is very sick. Youth workers also learn that young people are stressed about having an age assessment or not being assessed at the correct level at college. They may have money concerns and find it hard to cope on a tight budget and need someone to talk to. Then there are those who feel guilty if they are doing well – or not doing well – when reflecting on the hardships their families are enduring back home.

A downside of youth services and clubs is that they are male-orientated with sporting activities. Girls are excluded from male activities and often there is hardly anything available for girls, who are directed towards church and religious types of communities to see if anything can be offered to them.

The youth workers I spoke to regularly bear the brunt of young people's frustrations when confronted with a lack of services. Some noted that social workers rarely visit their projects. Some young people weren't even given their social worker's mobile number. So when a foster placement is in jeopardy of breaking down or another serious concern arises and requires urgent attention, some youth workers I spoke to have had little option but to refer concerns to external advocacy agencies, as opposed to Children's Services.

I also garnered views from these professionals about what they thought was working well in the system for young asylum seekers, as well as the negative factors, and this was the outcome.

## Positives

» There is a fairly good, structured system in place for asylum seekers and refugees in the UK (local authorities, charities, Home Office).

» Asylum seekers and refugees receive free healthcare and education.

» They also have access to free legal aid (in the initial part of their application and/or appeal).

## Negatives

» The asylum system is linear, in the sense that inconsistency arises in various parts of the country in terms of whether somebody gets a good social worker, personal adviser or solicitor and judge (appeal cases).

» Life is hard if somebody is placed in a small town or an area where there is racism or negative attitudes towards asylum seekers.

» Being subject to an incorrect age assessment is something that can negatively change the course of somebody's life – or even destroy it.

Horrific examples are relayed where young people attending school have had age assessments where they were assessed as being an adult – only for it to be later reversed and they get re-assessed back to being a youth. But during this time, it is not uncommon for that young person to lose their school placement. Similar decisions have also resulted in foster placements being taken away before getting placed in a shared house along with adults. I was told one story about a 15-year-old boy who was age assessed as being 25, until the decision was reversed back to his original age. In addition to losing his school and foster placement, and having to move to a completely different area where he knew nobody, he ended up getting arrested. Apparently, text messages on his phone revealed he had texted a 15-year-old girl at his school. The veil of suspicion fell on him being an adult texting a child with the intention of grooming her for sex – when in actual fact it was just an innocent exchange of text messages between school friends. The impact that wrong outcomes can have on lives is overwhelming, frightening and not morally defensive by any means. I will return to the subject of age assessments in Chapter 5.

# Integration

Young asylum seekers and refugees are brilliant networkers. They seek out others from their home communities and, together, they support each other. Owing to their shared experiences and common bonds, they become 'asylum' families. Sometimes there is little opportunity for asylum seekers and refugees to integrate into British society for systemic reasons mainly connected to language and cultural norms. But within communities – for example, Kurdish or Eritrean – they often behave like siblings and form strong bonds. One minute they are the best of friends and the next they hate each other!

It is not unusual for young people from Muslim countries to have a dogma of what is right or wrong, especially around issues concerning the LGBT community, women and how they dress and behave, as well as matters of intimacy and contraception. Sometimes there is friction in discussions involving Afghan people and those from Iraq and Iran. The same sometimes applies for those from Eritrea, Sudan and Ethiopia. But prejudice is often overcome by discussion and a willingness to appreciate various points of view that may not be accepted or tolerated in the young person's country of origin. They sometimes have to learn what equality and respect means. A prime example of this includes young people who are discriminatory towards LGBT people but then reach a point in their own lives where they become friends with a gay person, question their own sexuality or are drawn towards experimenting after they have become close to somebody of the same gender.

With regard to racism and discrimination, it is often only when a young person experiences these themselves that they begin to realise the impact this has on individual lives. Young asylum seekers and refugees sometimes find it difficult to make English friends at school and college. Discriminatory stories exist of how some young asylum seekers have wanted to socialise with white British friends outside of school or college, but were refused access to family homes after parents questioned where they came from and why, if they used drugs, or if they were violent or were sympathetic towards terrorist ideology. Interpretation is mainly embedded in education and foster care, and does not extend outwards to the broader community. Some other UASC don't even try to integrate and just remain friends within their own communities or with other young asylum seekers and refugees, but this often results in social isolation.

Religion is important to UASC in comparison to indigenous children of the same age. Yet it is often noticed that religious leaders are not involved in the lives of young people and are noticeably absent from professional meetings. Why is that? Many professionals have commented that imams and Christian ministers are reluctant to get involved with UASC, owing to time restraints as well as some being fearful that they will be asked for money. There is so much good work they could do – including inviting UASC to get involved in youth groups run by mosques and churches, many of which organise sporting activities like football and cricket.

# Universal Credit

Before the roll-out of Universal Credit in 2018, young care leavers over the age of 18 with LTR status were eligible to apply for Income Support. They were also able to work up to 16 hours a week without it affecting their benefits. That all changed when it was replaced by Universal Credit in what was intended to be a seamless process but still sometimes ends up being a difficult one for young people aged 18 or over. The initial application is fairly easy, but if a young person is unable to prove their identity online then they will be asked to attend an identity interview at the job centre. They also have to attend a further Habitual Residence Test at the Department for Work and Pensions (DWP), which is then followed by a separate interview, whereby the young person has to provide evidence of their learning agreement (if they attend college) and a tenancy/occupancy agreement confirming their accommodation.

The Universal Credit system is not well equipped at recognising care leavers, nor does it understand their circumstances. All UASC and young people come under the category of 'High Likely Need'. Payments are paid monthly (by default), but can be changed to an alternative payment agreement, eg fortnightly, upon request. The most incredible aspect of Universal Credit is that it pays the young person's rent into their bank accounts, along with their personal allowances, with the idea that the young person gives the rent money directly to their landlord. Some young people who receive these rent payments will contact their personal adviser; others spend the money and there is often no recourse. In order to avoid this pitfall from reoccurring, the personal adviser has to sign a declaration form requesting that funds are paid directly to the landlord.

The rationale behind Universal Credit is that it is supposed to prove that everybody is better off working than remaining on benefits – although, for some young people, this is not always apparently evident, with some feeling they are disadvantaged by the amount they pay. Those in consistent employment relinquish 63 pence out of every pound irrespective of how many hours worked – although they are able to inform DWP if their circumstances change because payments are made monthly and in arrears. Professionals fear this deduction may mean many young people choose cash-in-hand payments rather than the legitimate route, leading to a pathway of unscrupulous employers and exploitation.

Some professionals working with refugees who are on Universal Credit are unimpressed, believing that it has created a pathway that young people may not be able to relinquish. They are not frontloaded with many choices, the main barrier being that those who work part time then appear less well off than when on previous benefit payments prior to the introduction of Universal Credit (ie Income Support or Jobseeker's Allowance). The worst-case scenario is that some young people may become disillusioned, to the point they get drawn towards criminality because they feel they will never be able to carve out a decent living in Britain. Worse still, there may be a minority of young people who become radicalised because they feel Britain has failed them.

Young people with refugee status are legitimately eligible to work and, therefore, their employers will pay their tax and National Insurance. It is advisable that once a young person starts employment, they contact the DWP and inform them of their employment. It has been known for a young person's monthly allowance and rent to suddenly stop if information from HMRC (Her Majesty's Revenue and Customs) is sent to the DWP without the young person having first notified them of a change in their circumstances – a prosecutable offence that could lead to a criminal conviction.

# Aspirations and affection

It is very hard for young people to build a new life in Britain. For some, it is like starting all over again. Many young people struggle with trust issues. Most don't have any family connections in the country. Several endure trauma (PTSD) or have bereavement issues. Others easily become re-traumatised by the immigration process and feel they are mocked by a system that doesn't deliver or believe them. One young Iranian person I spoke to, who was waiting an exceptionally lengthy time for his substantive Home Office interview, said to me, *'The system is laughing at me... Why is my life a joke to these people?'* In addition to all this worry, stress and anxiety, young people are bombarded with meetings, new faces, schools or colleges, solicitors and social care and health professionals. Young people come to Britain with a perception of the country, particularly of London. Then they see London and often experience resentment and disappointment, realising that it is a big and lonely place for those without money.

All young people have aspirations to do well and get good jobs. But their lives become entangled for three reasons.

1. Trauma – the impact of trauma.

2. Separation from family and peers – feeling guilty for leaving their families behind.

3. Exhaustion – after much travelling at night, their body clock/rhythm is in considerable need of sleep and proper food.

In terms of the young people who struggle the most, this depends on an individual's circumstances before they arrived in the country, along with the suffering and hardship they endured during the journey. These factors all impact on their success in the UK and the young person's ability to survive. Young people who particularly struggle include those from Vietnam, who tend to be less outspoken. However, they are well supported and have a strong community base. They write better than they speak and isolate themselves from others because of that. Some young people from

Sudan may speak a dialect that few others speak or understand, resulting in them having fewer friends in their community.

In terms of expressing affection, the relationships between young people and foster carers are sometimes complicated. When it works well, though, it produces many positive outcomes, with genuine bonds of trust and love being formed. Some foster carers remain in touch with young refugees after they leave the placement and invite them back for Christmas or ask them to join them on family holidays. But ordinary day-to-day affections (hugs) are lacking because of professional boundaries – which equally applies to all professionals working with young people. These young people are left, therefore, to find affection and love from friends and in their communities. Many young people who are in relationships, or who are considering dating somebody, have remarked that there was nobody significant in their lives (parents or siblings) to approve of these relationships and they often revert to illicit relationships that need no approval. There are some sex-education classes (gender-separated groups) run by some charities and delivered by professionals who are unknown to the young people, which enables them to be open and non-judgemental.

Young people know the differences between paid professionals (social workers and 18plus personal advisers) and charity agencies (workers and volunteers who are not part of commissioned services). They know the latter is not bound by the duties and regulation of statutory services, which is why young people often turn to them when seeking advice, solace and support – practical and emotional. Language barriers also escalate when things are not properly explained by interpreters. Charity workers often notice how busy and stressed (or lazy) social workers can be, and that they fail to give their mobile numbers to young people – leaving them with nobody to help them in a crisis. Many young people are tenacious enough to battle through the difficulties.

Some young people battle with dyslexia and dyspraxia but have been timed out of the system, having reached the age of 18 before their additional needs are spotted. Local authorities need to be much more advanced at developing early intervention and devise a programme so that learning needs are identified sooner rather than later. A young person's sleep, diet and distress scale (trauma) also needs to be taken into consideration. Professionals need to find out more about the young person's life and what they want to achieve in their future. They need to be given support in the early stages of coming here, to encourage motivation and long-term success. All of this will assist in integration and make them feel valued both in general society and their own diaspora communities.

These young people need to be helped to develop resilience to feel good about themselves and with education, making friends and having hobbies. Ultimately, every young person needs to be viewed as an individual. Admittedly, asylum-seeking young people are sometimes more complex than citizen children, but there should not be any marked difference in their level of – or entitlement to – healthcare or education. While they often have to be given more consideration to bring them up to a 'starting point' in education and language, this should be viewed as their right and entitlement rather than a hindrance.

In terms of discrimination, those mistreated by professionals and services don't want to complain, because they think they will be seen as troublemakers and that it will affect services and their Home Office claim. Crowther (2019, p 81) sums this up well.

*If people who have left behind discrimination and persecution find themselves limited to an under-class existence here, we can hardly claim to have given them refuge. Sadly, refugees often accept discrimination as normal. But they don't have to.*

Many young people want to give back and are very generous in their nature. Some want to volunteer or take up training in social care. Some have expressed an interest in social work as a career. They want to reclaim agency and have control and ownership over their lives. That's why it's vitally important for young people to get as much help and support during their earlier years in the UK as possible, in order to manifest the best possible outcomes for their futures.

# Conclusion

If a group of young asylum seekers and refugees from various locations were gathered together, I think they would easily be able to showcase inconsistencies in services and provisions in relation to what each had received since coming to the UK. This might be a simple case of a young person living within a local authority in an affluent area that has a relatively small number of asylum seekers in their care. Imagine the difference between being placed in an independent fostering agency under such provision, compared to a local authority in a working-class district that has to take care of a few thousand young asylum seekers. The difference would be significant. The same would apply with the quality of shared independent accommodation and general services, namely youth facilities, colleges and employment opportunities for those with refugee status.

Imagine life for those over 18 – either with support from the leaving care team or other adults not entitled to this service (based on the age they entered the country). Services are reliant on funding and budgets, which are rarely the same two years running, based on political initiatives and directives from local authorities. Overall, it shows a system with widespread inconsistency in its services and duty of care to the vulnerable in society, and a system that stands on a perpetually shaky foundation.

# Chapter 4 | Trauma

# Introduction

Britain is often a country where young people are given psychiatric labels and over-diagnosed with mental health conditions before being placed on often dangerous and needless mind-altering psychotropic medication. This is a country where the service responsible for treating the emotional well-being of children and young people – the Child and Adolescent Mental Health Service (CAMHS) – is not fit for purpose after decades of catastrophic failure owing to insufficient resources, long waiting lists and often ineffective interventions.

Before I started working with young asylum seekers and refugees, I expected this particular population of young people to suffer from several emotional and mental health issues owing to the horrific experiences they had to navigate through before arriving in the UK, not least the journey to actually get here in the first place. But, to my surprise, the young people I encountered over a two-year period did not, in the main, exhibit signs of mental distress. Contrary to what I expected, I found that the vast majority of these young people were healthy, happy, emotionally stable and resilient – except for a handful who showed signs of mild anxiety and self-reported sleep difficulties.

I have come to discover, however, that while young people may look fine on a daily basis, they are not because they have underlying encapsulated trauma that will never go away by itself. Their demeanour may appear cheerful at college or work, but they are often inwardly distressed. Many are just not at the point where they are ready to deal with their feelings. The trauma is buried deep within them and may not manifest itself until rekindled by a new traumatic event – or during the natural process of brain aging. The key, though, is to identify trauma and name it.

# Acknowledging trauma

Psychiatric professionals have advised that every young asylum seeker and refugee should be considered as having trauma or PTSD until proven otherwise. They also recommend that professionals working with them look closely for symptoms, because they will find them if they do so. This doesn't imply that every young person will be diagnosed with PTSD, but rather that every child will have some symptoms of trauma because all of them have been exposed to it at some point or other during their lives. All refugee and asylum-seeking children and young people are likely to have experienced trauma within the country from which they fled, during their journey from this country to the one in which they seek refuge and on arrival in their host country. Issues of loss may be exacerbated by a lack of support systems, such as family and community life, and the associated isolation.

It is strange but true to realise that all the big things going on in the world at the current time – whether it's war, poverty, climate change or terrorism – will have impacted on lives of UASC children in the UK to one degree or another. These young people will have experienced more hardship, suffering and unsettlement before the age of 18 than their counterpart citizen children will encounter in their entire lives. That is a daunting thought, but it is true. Yet, not enough emphasis is placed on the emotional suffering of young people who are often not treated as favourably as citizen children by professionals, including mental health professionals, based on a shortage of resources, cultural and language differences and personally held political views.

There are many reasons why young asylum seekers and refugees become stressed, anxious, depressed and overwhelmed by life in the UK. Trauma may emerge due to:

» childhood experiences – death, abuse (physical, emotional, sexual and neglect), domestic violence, and mental illness in parents and/or other family members;

» the long application process to get refugee status (LTR), resulting in life being in limbo coupled with an inability to plan the future;

» language difficulties – and the stress of not being understood;

» being asked long streams of questions by various professionals (why did you come here, what happened during your journey?);

» shame of the past and feelings of inadequacy as they embark on life in a new country amongst a different culture;

» a lack of trust in authority – or having been abused by the authority in the past – and fear of information being passed onto authorities in their home countries;

» the feeling of a loss of purpose in life;

» the inability to feel a sense of belonging in the UK;

» feelings of unworthiness, owing to being sexually abused in their home countries or en route to the UK;

» attachment difficulties in childhood, which has resulted in episodes of self-harming behaviour to help elevate stress and frustration;

» the feeling of wanting to run away from everything and everyone because of thoughts that nobody cares.

Experts state that 80 per cent of young people can process painful memories without lasting effect, while 20 per cent are unable to cope with the traumatic memories that flood their minds. In such cases, their behaviour is often described as being easily triggered, displaying uncontrollable actions that are accompanied with disorganised thoughts and vivid sensory information as a result of the lingering effects of their trauma. These young people need to be helped to realise that what happened did so in the past and that it is not happening now. They need to learn how to train their brains to segregate the difference and this can only be achieved by working with psychologists or professionals who are trained in trauma. Some young people will have ignored the trauma for many years and will suffer from trauma-causing memories as a result.

Most of these young people are in a toxic stress state because the trauma has overwhelmed them. They don't understand their emotional state and do not have the vocabulary to articulate or describe their feelings. It is harder to recover from toxic stress when surrounded by people who are suffering in the same way. This is hard given that a large percentage of young asylum seekers and refugees live together or gravitate to other young people from their respective communities. As a result, this places them in situations where they have a reduced ability to self-regulate (the capability to control behaviour, emotions and thoughts) and have a reduced ability to make sense of the world. They may also have impaired social functioning as a result.

Home Office substantive interviews, which decide whether young people get their LTR, are often very traumatic. The questions often bring up old issues and memories. In addition to this, these young people have to tell their story repeatedly. There is often no trauma recognition in the methods used by the Home Office, which are often conducted in a hostile way and with an 'I don't believe'-type of attitude. If something in their past is so painful, it will prevent them from telling their story. They are not lying by saying they can't remember certain events – their disorganised brains mix up snippets of information and facts and their stories often don't make sense because they are unable to understand the trauma that occurred.

In essence, staff at the Home Office are not trauma-informed so, therefore, it is essential for social workers to sensitively inform their young people of the procedures and not keep them in the dark. Support is vital in this area and it is essential to prepare the young people for a negative outcome. Furthermore, it is important for social workers to inform legal representatives of the emotional health of their young people, and be prepared to write a letter to the Home Office outlining what needs to be made known about their mental state and what impact this is having on their lives.

# Trauma in young people

The UK today has thousands of young asylum seekers and refugees living in its towns and cities. These young people are all battling aspects of trauma to some extent. Research by Lewis et al (2019) and published in *The Lancet Psychiatry* stated that for citizen children, one in three experience trauma in childhood and are thereby being affected by toxic stress that leads to emotional injury. Furthermore, one in 12 children meet the diagnostic criteria for PTSD, owing to a clinically significant level of distress affecting their everyday life. Given these statistics, it is hard to imagine that citizen children – born in a country devoid of war, famine and persecution – could compare to the experiences of asylum-seeking children and young people who have had to endure inhumane, cruel and often intolerable suffering and hardship.

Many young asylum seekers' lives are uncertain as they wait to have their Home Office substantive interview to determine whether or not they receive their initial five-year LTR in the country. Many will not feel safe until they get their LTR. They will feel like they are stuck and can't move forward in life. Those who do receive their LTR, however, are still not free from uncertainty. Most have no idea where their families are and many feel lost and abandoned in a country where they can stay for a fixed period before being able to apply for permanency. Without family contact and having a sense of belonging, lives are sometimes dismal and lived without hope or joy.

Most of these young people are either suffering from trauma or PTSD or fall within the lower threshold of an official diagnosis – referred to as sub-threshold PTSD, in the sense they exhibit many of its symptoms but have not been assessed and given an official diagnosis. Psychiatric experts consider this applies to every asylum and refugee child. They even suggest a significant percentage will have diagnosable PTSD and a large percentage will encounter symptoms related to PTSD, although ongoing research is being carried out to verify the validity of this claim. Moreover, it is suggested that some young asylum seekers and refugees will display signs of having a mental disorder, including personality disorder (which I will address later in this chapter).

As previously mentioned, these young people have been overwhelmed so often that it is felt they have blocked out emotions. This results in them presenting as emotionally healthy after they become absorbed in other ways, keeping their real feelings hidden underneath the surface. Psychiatrists refer to them as having dissociated themselves from the painful memories that are stored in their brains, unprocessed. However, as they journey through late adolescence and into early adulthood, life events will eventually trigger emotional distress and bring it to the surface. Therefore, it is best to get the trauma treated as soon as possible, allowing the young people to grow into adults who move forward in their lives and thrive in key areas such as relationships and employment. The main point to remember here is that is it possible to recover from trauma, but some young people will need extra help with their emotional injuries and therefore referrals to specialist agencies will need to take place.

# The Norway study

UASC are known to be subjected to several life events that potentially risk their mental health significantly more than citizen children of the same age. They encounter numerous risk factors that can cause psychological distress, including exposure to violence and multiple losses. It is also recognised that UASC come from countries with a history of war and weak social fabric, with frequent exposure to loss and trauma, limited access to healthcare and social adversities in their upbringing.

Research from Norway by Jakobsen et al (2014) was the largest piece of research carried out on UASC. It studied 160 male children, who were assessed and interviewed by means of symptom checklists and trauma questionnaires, along with questions about stressful life events. It was found that most of those interviewed had experienced negative life events including torture, loss of a close relative, serious injury, combat, natural disaster, war-related experiences, physical abuse, sexual abuse, forced separation, witnessing life threat and violence against others, and/or the murder of a family member. The study found that 41.9 per cent of the children fulfilled the diagnostic criteria for a current psychiatric disorder – while 30 per cent of all of the children in the study showed symptoms prevalent in the diagnosis of PTSD The study's findings concluded that UASC are a very vulnerable group with a high prevalence of psychiatric morbidity. Those interviewed had experienced numerous threatening, horrible and potentially traumatic events, including bereavement, and overall they lacked the protection and social stability that parents could have offered. In addition to the high prevalence of PTSD, the study found that depression and anxiety disorders were also quite common.

# Diagnostic criteria

There is a revolution going on in the world of mental health, at present, between psychiatrists and psychologists who are discovering more and more about the effects of PTSD in young asylum seekers and refugees. PTSD was first introduced in 1980 by the American Psychiatric Association, and it was previously known as war neurosis, shell shock and nervous shock. Social workers and other professionals working with these young people need to be equipped to recognise the signs and symptoms of PTSD, but only psychiatrists and clinical psychologists are able to officially diagnose the condition. There are two main diagnostic manuals used in psychiatry to diagnosis PTSD: *The Diagnostic and Statistical Manual of Mental Disorders (DSM-5)*, compiled by the American Psychiatric Association (APA), and the *International Classification of Diseases (ICD-11)*, compiled by the World Health Organization (WHO). Both manuals share more similarities than differences.

To make an official diagnosis, an assessment-style questionnaire consisting of 30 pages is completed. This may take several hours because it extensively examines symptoms, trauma history and attachment history. The psychiatrist or psychologist completing the questionnaire may provide psycho-education to the young person about how the brain works and the reasons for sleeplessness and anxiety. It will also help the young person realise that they are otherwise an adjusted young person who has been through an overwhelming experience. This will help them understand themselves a lot more and enable them to realise that their brain just hasn't been able to process the trauma they experienced.

In order for somebody to be diagnosed with PTSD they need to directly experience or witness a traumatic event, or learn that a traumatic event has happened to a close family member or friend and to experience repeated or extreme exposure to details of the traumatic event (either hearing details from family members or seeing media reports related to the event). People suffering from PTSD may be affected by continuously re-experiencing the event with thoughts or perceptions relating to it. This may include flashbacks and images and dreams or nightmares that reference the event. During periods of stress, they may experience illusions or hallucinations, and there will be times when they may even experience intense distress or reaction to cues that symbolise some aspect of the event.

Other criteria that can be found in those suffering from PTSD include an inability to remember an important aspect of the event or having enduring and exaggerated negative beliefs about themselves, others and the world. They might present in a persistent negative emotional state, with a diminished interest or participation in activities they previously liked and found enjoyable. They may also drop out of college or stop working. Being in this negative state of mind will also entail having persistent distorted thoughts about the causes or the consequences of the event, accompanied with feelings of detachment or estrangement from others. Overall, there will be a distinct inability to experience positive emotions in any aspect of life.

PTSD presents in various manifestations consisting of either avoidance or reactions. The former entails avoiding thoughts, feelings or conversations associated with the event. Avoiding people, places or activities that may trigger recollections is also a prominent feature. When confronted, or likely to be confronted, with events, people or discussions that are considered likely triggers, people with PTSD will often respond with irritable behaviour and angry outbursts. They can display hypervigilance (constantly on the lookout for signs of potential danger) or exhibit an exaggerated startle response (jumping at the slightest sound). They may also have concentration problems or sleep problems, or both. Finally, they might display reckless or self-destructive behaviour, including the misuse of alcohol and drugs, promiscuous sex or get involved in criminal activities.

Psychiatrists have also discovered that young people with PSTD will often present with dissociation, whereby traumatic memories will remain floating around in the brain and be triggered by events and people. This type of trauma is often referred to as dissociative trauma and often manifests itself through daydreaming, which is deemed as a kind of depersonalisation and a removal from everyday reality. Although some young people will have different tolerance thresholds when in a dissociative state, others can present as being very impulsive, have frequent panic attacks, be very controlling, exhibit self-harming behaviour or fly into rages easily. Ultimately, they will be unable to thrive. Dissociation is a barrier to the pain of arousal. They may sleep a lot, but not feel rested upon waking. Trauma disrupts thinking and is tinged with fears and anxiety. It is essential to remember, though, that young asylum seekers and refugees will have been traumatised in their mother tongue and many will have had to learn a new language since arriving in Britain.

In very severe cases, the dissociation will be so overwhelming that the young people will not have memories of the various significant events that happened in their lives, to the point it resembles amnesia. It can take on feelings of numbness and illusion in the young person, making them feel empty or unreal – to the point they may be unable to connect with other people and present as cold, uncaring, aloof and/or overly pre-occupied with themselves.

Of course, recognising symptoms of PTSD in young people is one thing, but getting them to realise how and why they are hurting emotionally is another. Furthermore, advising them to engage with the professional services that will assist recovery and help them reconcile with the horrendous events of their past is something else altogether. Young people who exhibit PTSD symptoms may prompt social workers to make a referral to CAMHS for assessment. Some will attend their assessments but many will refuse to engage, mainly as a result of cultural attitudes about seeking help for mental health. Many originate from countries where issues pertaining to mental illness are considered taboo. In Iraq, for example, there is only one mental hospital for a population of 38 million people. Young people from countries that are predominantly Islamic, as well as those from African countries, have rarely heard constructive conversations about mental health services. This is reflected in young people fearing discussion and/or being labelled unwell or insane, whereby they often exclaim, '*I'm not mad*' when referrals to specialist services are suggested.

# Social work intervention

UASC and young people often experience various traumas rather than one singular event. Some have been overwhelmed many times in their lives, with some having reached the point where they are no longer able to deal with the painful emotions attached to memories. In such times, they react in two ways and either become hypo (becoming quiet or silent) or hyper (becoming vocal or angry). The brain can heal itself because there is capacity in it to understand complex narratives. When young people better understand their trauma, they have a better chance of healing.

Young people spend a lot of time with their social workers; hence, it's imperative they are treated sensitively and with care. Social workers who are trauma-informed have a better chance of helping young people in their care. The more trauma-informed they are, the more pitfalls they will avoid. Social workers need to be empathetic and not display a rushed or 'not bothered' approach when speaking to young people about their life stories. Admittedly, this can be hard to achieve if the social worker is stressed or experiencing burnout (emotional drainage due to constantly giving and not receiving), but the essential thing to know is that whatever approach the social worker uses will affect how the young person responds.

# Aarash (17) from Afghanistan

*After his parents and younger brothers were killed in an airstrike, Aarash's uncle arranged for him to leave the country. Aarash first tried cannabis when he 'lived' in Istanbul, which was the first place he settled in after leaving Afghanistan. He stayed there for two years, aimlessly walking around during the day to combat the boredom. Although Aarash liked the city and the seafront, he survived on little money until a friend introduced him to some men who were rumoured to be good at helping people. At first, the men appeared friendly. They offered food, advice and promises of finding a way to get Aarash to Germany – maybe even Britain. It was during one of these visits that one of the men touched Aarash's genitals and made him do things that made him feel uncomfortable. Money and supplies of hashish made him continue meeting the man until he had saved enough money to leave Turkey. Aarash eventually ended up in Dover, concealed in the back of a lorry.*

*Life in Britain proved difficult. School was a real challenge, with Aarash finding it a struggle to sit in class and concentrate. He began missing school and then stopped going altogether. Then he met a girl he really liked. They dated for a few months, until one day Aarash found his girlfriend kissing another boy. He got very angry and shouted and swore at both of them. His trust had been broken. To ease his sorrow, he smoked more cannabis than usual, to the point where he didn't have to think about anything or anyone anymore. It also made him feel better and lifted his pain. Thoughts of returning to Afghanistan clouded his mind. He wondered if he could return and find his uncle. Maybe he could have a good life there now that the country had begun to stabilise. Aarash also dreamed of marriage and children, so that he could have his own family. These were his daydreams while he smoked cannabis, day after day.*

Social workers are often the ones who build up the closest relationships with young refugees and they are often first to spot the signs and identify behaviours connected to trauma. They are the ones who look out for psychological disturbances and are educated in this field. Social workers are invariably highly skilled professionals but, even so, need to be trauma-informed and trained in recognising red flags in young people. Social workers are often the first point of contact in the lives of young refugees and often the first to meet new arrivals. They need to make these young people feel safe after their horrible ordeal of travelling to the UK, and know their emotional struggles and what to look out for. They need to be aware that these young people will have experienced trauma both in their country of origin and during their journey to the UK, and that they will also experience trauma and difficulties settling into a new country far away from family and friends, familiar cultural surroundings and climatic differences.

Social workers must ask the young people how they are feeling and acknowledge their responses. They must glean as much information as they can about their lives and backgrounds, in the most sensitive way possible, before deciding where best to place them. This may be in foster care, semi-independent accommodation or in a shared independent living placement. It is imperative the young people are made to feel that the people in charge are on their side and making the best decisions for them, because often the system they are entering is restricted by resources and financial constraints.

A certain number of young UASC will arrive with obvious PTSD symptoms, such as displaying high anxiety and stress levels coupled with erratic sleep patterns. Social workers, foster carers and care staff often don't understand what is going on in the minds of these young people. They might think that they are playing up or are being ungrateful for the help and support they are being given. Changes in attitudes towards school or college or a drop in attendance – one minute doing well and then changing the next – as well as shifts in behaviour in their home environment are also key signs that that the young person is struggling. Social workers need to know when to intervene after determining that the behaviour exceeds that associated with normal adolescent behaviour. They need to know that UASC are the same as every other young person – that in addition to enduring trauma as a result of their circumstances, they are also dealing with adolescence as well. This is a challenging time, especially for boys whose testosterone levels are 30 times higher during puberty than normal.

Insufficient funding and resources place greater pressure on social workers to fill the gap, which could lead to unfair responsibility being placed on them to become quasi 'therapists'. There will always be social workers who are empathic to the needs of their clients and do a good job, but equally there will be others who are less sensitive – with the added risk of assuming the role of an untrained 'voyeuristic' therapist, who risks doing far more harm than good. Finally, anti-discriminatory practice isn't always applied in social work, because there will always be some social workers who lack affinity towards asylum seekers and refugees. Some hold political views supporting the idea that the UK is overcrowded and has too many refugees, and that this has put pressure on the system and taken resources away from citizen children and families. Sadly, this raises its head more than it is acknowledged and it needs addressing in order for there to be a much healthier attitude towards young asylum seekers and refugees.

Secondary trauma impacts on social workers and affects them all in some way or other. Certain young people will bring it up with the social worker and how it is managed is important. It needs to be recognised and addressed through training on trauma and learning to self-regulate. This can be achieved either through support from colleagues or in group clinical supervision – or more informally through the support of family and friends. In severe cases, personal therapy may be advisable if the impact of the trauma is prolonged. But the key point is – *it is the trauma that is the problem and not the child.*

## Dalmar (16) from Somalia

*Dalmar lost an eye in a childhood accident. He was conscious about the way he looked. He had one or two friends, but found it hard to socialise with people he didn't know. Many in his social circle viewed him differently and often joked about him behind his back, finding fault with his misunderstanding of some English words, the way he dressed or his views of the world. Some were particularly cruel and called him 'stupid' and 'backward'.*

*Dalmar was obsessed with security. At home, he constantly checked windows and doors to ensure nobody could break into the house while he was asleep. Others living in the house would have preferred locks on their bedroom doors to preserve privacy, but Dalmar did not fuss over this, preferring to leave his bedroom door ajar at night-time to ensure he would hear anybody attempting to break into the house. He would remain vigilant until he fell asleep.*

*Dalmar missed his family back in Somalia, and they missed him too. He found the occasional phone call to them reassuring. He was the eldest in a family of six. His father died when he was a young boy, leaving him the man in charge of the house and family. There were very few comforting things in his life. He rarely thought about the future and didn't have any dream or plan, which meant he stayed in bed on the days he wasn't attending his ESOL course.*

*Dalmar didn't seem to have anything to look forward to. But he did like singing in secret and, when his housemates weren't home, he often secretly filmed himself on his phone doing one of his favourite rap songs. He didn't dare show these clips to anybody, fearful of their criticism, and, although he felt a little awkward seeing himself on screen when he played it back, he also felt a certain sense of achievement at the same time.*

Nobody expects social workers or other care professionals to be medical experts, but it is useful to have some understanding of the brain and how it can heal itself after trauma. There are several parts of the brain worth knowing about as follows: first, the ventrolateral prefrontal cortex is a region of the brain that's involved in self-regulatory processes, such as the damping down of impulsive emotions like fear and anger, which becomes impaired after trauma. Second, the amygdala shuts down the frontal lobes during traumatic flashbacks while, third, the hippocampus, which plays an important role in storing information from short-term memory to long-term memory, is affected after traumatic experiences. It is useful for social workers to be confident to discuss with clients what thought or belief helped them to cope with their ordeal and what got them through their experience, and it is important to acknowledge their survival and make them realise their resilience. In doing so, this will help young people put their story into a meaningful narrative and ensure it is in context. It will also enable them to realise that what happened was outside of their control.

Traumatised young people will experience images popping into their awareness, emotional switching from happy to sad, and body sensations, as well as thoughts and beliefs that they are going to die. Young people think about their experiences much of the time. It lurks in the background and is stored in the hippocampus. Some young people find it extremely difficult to settle because they are full of guilt or shame, blaming themselves for situations and circumstances, such as being unable to find their families, or feeling guilty about being separated from parents during their journeys, which they think was their fault.

Social workers are often faced with two hard tasks. In today's work practice, they are often *de facto* counsellors, expected to help young people navigate between 'inner' and 'outer' worlds – aiding their recovery from past traumas, while coping with life in a new country. A gap has to be bridged between these two distinct factors to create a safe environment in the present. Social workers may have heard the same or similar background story from several of their young people, and while some of this is coincidental, it is also a falsehood being replayed from the 'pitch' given by agents who instruct young people on what to say when they arrive in the UK. But it is necessary to move beyond these background stories. The young people need to be seen, first and foremost, as children who are often frightened, alone and confused when they enter the UK, not knowing what to expect.

Young people need lots of help and reassurance while they wait for Home Office decisions, and it often rests upon social workers to provide this support. A compassionate heart is needed. There are many activities that social workers can signpost young people to take part in including sports and other means of physical exercise, as well as breathing exercises, yoga and mindfulness to help with panic attacks and hypervigilance. Social workers will also be the first to spot signs of drug and alcohol misuse, which young people with PTSD may resort to as a coping mechanism. It is not unusual for some to self-medicate with cannabis or cocaine – although, on the whole, numbers are still relatively low owing to cultural and religious factors.

## Shakeel (17) from Iran

*At all times, in all seasons, Shakeel would complain of feeling cold, even when indoors. It didn't matter if the central heating was on full capacity, he would still sometimes shiver and complain of not feeling warm enough. During periods of exceptionally hot weather in the summer, Shakeel would carry a jacket in his rucksack, just in case he needed to wear it. Sometimes he blamed the English climate. At other times, he recognised that the feeling of always being cold started during a leg of his journey to the UK. During this time, he was once positioned next to a large refrigerator unit in the back of the lorry. He remembers getting out of the lorry, in either Italy or France, and being completely numb with cold, to the point he had to keep rubbing his hands to get feeling back into them.*

*Shakeel suffered terribly from nightmares. Every week he had at least one nightmare before waking up trembling and sweating. He mainly had two recurring dreams. In one dream, he was always running away from a building that he expected to be blown up; in the other dream, he would be walking across a narrow platform above the sea, feeling completely exposed and petrified that he would fall. In both dreams, the fear felt so real that when he woke up it took several minutes before he realised it was just a dream and his fears were allayed.*

*Preparing for the Home Office interview caused Shakeel much anxiety. He fretted over the questions he would get asked and feared not being able to answer them. In fact, anxiety featured heavily as his modus operandi in life, whether this was concerning his legal status, where he lived and who he lived with, college, money, family or the future. Shakeel knew that other young people didn't worry as much as he did, but dismissed their carefree attitude. However, he always sought out other people from his community to ask for advice, even for the smallest of problems, which he mulled over in great depth until he was satisfied he had been given the correct answer.*

# Treatments for trauma

Young people are rarely eager to engage in counselling-style treatments, but none more so than UASC and young people. There are a few reasons for this, one of which is language barriers. Having to discuss intimate details through an interpreter, who may be judgemental and aloof to the young person's life story, is a massive deterrent. Different cultures fear the mental illness label and abstain from anybody or any place where this is associated. There is the added dimension of the young person feeling that they will be able to manage their problems (trauma) by themselves and don't need help from others. However, psychotherapy, cognitive behaviour therapy (CBT) and medication are the three main sources of help offered when clinical diagnoses of PTSD take place.

## Psychotherapy

During psychotherapy, the therapist finds the main trigger point and gets the client to talk over their story repeatedly. Every young person has a 'hotspot' where their trauma has been ignored in events that happened that were totally outside their control. Young people with trauma react in many different ways and either exhibit a 'flight or fight' or a 'freeze or flop' response as a way of dealing with their emotions. Many will experience flashbacks of the event and that causes the highest level of trauma. It may involve memories of life-threatening events, witnessing or enduring severe injury, physical or sexual abuse, near-death experiences, witnessing suicide or death or being close to somebody who died.

In PTSD there is always an avoidance of something, related to the original event, which manifests itself in the young person's consciousness when they are faced with reminders in everyday life. Avoidance of things (including people and certain conversations) becomes routine, because they know that re-experiencing an event means they will have to deal with the pain, variances in mood and/or disrupted sleep patterns. Mood changes may include depression, anxiety, worry or a sense of doom. Young people with trauma may also be hypervigilant; hearing a knock on the door will make them jump because of the elevated nervous system they have developed.

It is believed that prolonged exposure over many sessions will help them realise they have survived and are coming out the other side. Furthermore, it is felt that post-trauma growth can't be achieved without exposure, although pressure must not be placed on the client to engage in counselling or give information about their lives that is painful. It is really important, therefore, that the therapist and the young person develop a strong and trusted rapport, and that the therapist is sensitive to the young person's needs at all times. This includes using a technique known as 'safety and stabilisations', where the therapist distracts the client if the memory becomes too painful by throwing them a pen to catch or asking them to count backwards. This will help the frontal lobes of the brain bring the young person back into the present time, along with restoring their breathing back to normal.

The most important detail to know about psychotherapy in the treatment of PTSD in young people is that there is an 80 per cent chance the therapist will help heal once they get to the unresolved emotional issue (hotspot). However, persistence is the key to success and the young person must be willing to engage fully by attending regular sessions to ensure the best outcome. The downside of psychotherapy is that many UASC fear divulging private information about themselves in front of interpreters, who they perceive as being judgemental. There are exceptionally long waiting lists to get a diagnosis and counselling at CAMHS, because of resource funding and the hiring of interpreters. The drop-out rate is high owing to the exposure and intensity of having to repeatedly go over traumatic experiences of the past.

## Cognitive behaviour therapy (CBT)

CBT is less intensive than psychotherapy and more commonly used to treat young people with trauma. Those with a clinical diagnosis are generally offered six to eight sessions of CBT on the National Health Service (NHS), which helps with narrative exposure. Like psychotherapy, CBT is a talking therapy that assists the young person with PTSD to better manage their problems by changing the way they think and behave.

CBT will help address avoiding feelings of hurt caused by the past, which is a common and central feature of PTSD. It will help the person face up to memories of a traumatic event and educate them around PTSD. CBT helps people deal with overwhelming problems by breaking them down into smaller parts. By doing so it is felt that physical feelings, thoughts and actions can be more closely looked at in order to determine how unhelpful these are and to look at ways of changing them. CBT can be very task-focused, with the therapist working through difficulties with the patient and ascertaining what actions need to be done to elicit change. The aim is to become more self-sufficient at recognising instructive thoughts and feelings and being able to self-regulate and self-heal.

CBT also provides guidance with general anxiety management. The patient may be assigned tasks to carry out in-between sessions and coping strategies will be offered (for example, with sleeping problems, advice will be given on regular sleep patterns when the whole body rhythm is out of place, avoiding energy drinks and regular tips like hot baths and avoiding tea and coffee before bedtime). Advice on the dangers of drug and alcohol misuse may also be included if these are areas of concern.

Sometimes CBT is tried on people when medication has failed to make a difference. The advantage of CBT over psychotherapy is that the therapy can be completed in a short period of time (sometimes within two to three months). However, the downside to CBT is that because it is a short-term treatment, it does not delve deep enough into long-term mental illnesses or address the root cause, such as an unhappy childhood.

## Mindfulness

Mindfulness, a form of meditation rooted in Buddhism, is becoming increasingly popular and is often used by the army to treat soldiers with PTSD. Mindfulness is about connecting and bringing balance to mind, body and emotions. Its aim is to train a person to become aware of, feel connected to and in touch with the present moment, as well as altering a person's relationship with their thoughts so they can realise that thoughts should be allowed to come and go.

Social workers probably already practise aspects of mindfulness with young people without realising. How common it is to encounter a young person in a stressful state, when the first reaction is to ask them to take a breath and calm down. Breath work plays a big part in mindfulness, whereby the person is asked to relax, close their eyes and pay attention to their bodily sensations, thoughts and emotions. Young people are accepting of new ideas and practices, and if the social worker has a good relationship with the young person, the better the chance they will have in getting the young person to comply, even if it is done initially in a jocular way.

Research on mindfulness is very promising. Boyd et al (2018) discovered it is effective in reducing the symptoms of PTSD and prevents depression. In essence, mindfulness tries to remove the fear of flashbacks and negative feelings from the past from occurring. However, it is not a therapy or a quick fix for trauma, and is best used alongside counselling or medication. It could, therefore, be implemented as a useful tool for social workers and 18plus personal advisers, provided they receive training in how to practise it with their young people.

## Medication

Many people with PTSD have very significant levels of depression. They may be tired, lack motivation, appear sad and show little interest in hobbies and education, coupled with a poor appetite that may entail weight loss. Some may even self-harm. A significant percentage of young asylum seekers and refugees displaying these types of 'symptoms' may be prescribed antidepressants if psychotherapy or CBT is not available in their area and there are extensive waiting lists at CAMHS. But anyone taking antidepressants has to take the tablets for three weeks before they see any signs of them working.

Putting a child on antidepressants should never be taken lightly, owing to the often dangerous and adverse side-effects these medications have on the central nervous system. Psychiatrists often dismiss these side-effects and may not even tell the young person or their carers about them (therefore preventing them from being able to make an informed choice). Instead, they may list the benefits of medication, eg reducing anxiety levels or helping to induce sleep. The antidepressants prescribed are mainly Selective Serotonin Reuptake Inhibitors (SSRIs), which are a class of drugs that are typically used in the treatment of major depressive disorder and anxiety disorders.

Antidepressants are mood-altering elevators, but do not solve the underlying emotional problem. Therefore, they will only mask the symptoms for as long as the patient takes the medication. Taking antidepressants can make some young people feel suicidal when they had not considered this before starting the medication. Suicidal feelings have mainly been associated with SSRIs. The list of other side-effects is very long and includes: nausea, weakness, headaches, indigestion, diarrhoea, loss of appetite, drowsiness, dizziness, anxiety, nervousness, shakiness (tremors), dry mouth, sweating, irregularities in heartbeat, flu-like symptoms, hot flashes, pins and needles feeling in head/extremities, weight gain, abdominal pain, tiredness/lack of energy, emotional numbness, irritability, akathisia (uncontrollable limb and body movements) and severe restlessness.

Antidepressants can also become highly addictive in a short length of time. Some young people become 'tolerant' to antidepressants after taking them for some time, resulting in the dosage having to be increased to maintain the original effect. There should be a withdrawal exit strategy in place from the very outset, before a child or young person starts taking medication. NICE (National Institute for Health and Care Excellence) guidelines recommend that a person should only be on medication for a set period of time (eg 12 months) before gradual withdrawal should take place. This rarely occurs and, unfortunately, addiction to antidepressants becomes commonplace. Anybody taking antidepressants must not stop taking them without medical advice; many experience withdrawal symptoms if abruptly stopped, resulting in having to go back on them.

In addition to antidepressants, some young people who exhibit anger management and irritability issues – because their body has been put into a state of heightened 'fight or flight' – or those who endure hallucinations during flashbacks, may be prescribed a low dosage of antipsychotic medication. Again, this medication has powerful side-effects and must not be prescribed without adequately informing the young person and carer about the consequences. An exit strategy should be in place from the beginning, to avoid long-term suffering and malfunctions from the side-effects attributed to the medication.

# Mental disorders

A number of young asylum seekers and refugees self-harm. This is an indicator that a personality disorder exists or is emerging; however, it is recognised that trauma affects personality change. Therefore, it is essential to treat the trauma and for the young person to learn coping skills, ie an ability to self-regulate and receive psycho-social guidance on trauma before exploration takes place that establishes more entrenched problems. Furthermore, it is also crucial to consider that personality disorders are primarily linked to trauma and attachment issues in childhood linked to the person's primary caregiver(s). Both these factors readily appear in many cases in relation to young asylum seekers and refugees, owing to their personal and environmental circumstances.

## Adjustment disorders

There is a thin line between adjustment disorders and PTSD, because the more severe cases are exactly the same as PTSD. Adjustment disorders will often present with considerable disturbance of emotion and are often referred to as complex PTSD when the young person presents with disorganised thoughts and disturbed emotions. It is therefore not uncommon to see people who are profoundly sad or have feelings of hopelessness. They may lack enjoyment, feel angry or guilty, experience insomnia or have difficulties with concentration. They may also have suicidal thoughts.

There is also a connection between adjustment disorders and attachment difficulties found in separated adolescents. In 1995, the Department of Health outlined in a document entitled *Unaccompanied Asylum-seeking Children* that: '*It is important to remember that despite the often traumatic circumstances surrounding the flight from their homeland the majority of these children are likely to have come from otherwise secure, stable family backgrounds.*' It was also considered by Groark et al (2011) that separation from a primary attachment figure can be painful and result in feelings of isolation and insecurity. Stabilisation is the first priority for these young people and a key part of this will need to be a consistent and available carer, such as a foster family, mentor or support worker. Once this level of 'stability' has been achieved, some young people will be able to make sense of their experiences, move on and build a new life for themselves.

There is also a strong connection between parents with PTSD and the emotional stability of their children, as a direct result of the parent's inability to form secure, healthy attachments with their children. Research carried out by van Ee et al (2016) in the Netherlands looked at adverse parenting and child attachment in a sample of 68 asylum seekers and refugees and their children (aged 18–42 months). The results showed that parental symptoms of PTSD were directly related to children's insecure and disorganised attachment. This was owing to poor or extremely insensitive parenting behaviour, which had affected the bond between child and parent at the most crucial and early stages of the children's development.

## Dissocial Identity Disorder (DID)

Dissocial Identity Disorder is a form of personality disorder. There is no solid evidence as to what causes a person to develop a personality disorder; however, trauma in childhood is often cited as a possible cause based on a core feature of those diagnosed. Abuse amounts to 90 per cent of cases with this diagnosis. The symptoms include *'the presence of two or more distinct personality states'*. This means that, on the one hand, a person can have great difficulty remembering key parts of their life, while on the other, they squash or avoid recalling events, people and circumstances owing to fear, shame and guilt. This often results in chaotic lives and an inability to form attachments with people. People with DID find it difficult to sustain relationships and have high degrees of distrust.

Childhood abuse is often found in young people with DID and linked to war, famine, persecution and dysfunctional parenting. There is a lot of anecdotal evidence about personality disorders. Some psychiatrists claim that a person with one will have at least one parent with a similar condition. People with personality disorders struggle in relationships, have trust issues and cannot form healthy attachments – all of which could pinpoint to factors in their childhood that caused them trauma and interfered with them developing trustful relationships with adults. In addition to PTSD being found in those with a diagnosis of DID, other problems that have arisen include depression, anxiety, substance misuse and self-harm.

Counselling is the most recommended treatment for both adjustment disorder and DID, although antidepressants could be prescribed for those suffering from deep depression. Psychiatrists state there is no cure for personality disorder – it is a lifelong condition. However, some people do eventually find equilibrium and respond well to people who deliver consistency while maintaining boundaries and respect.

# Conclusion

It is estimated that in ten years' time, greater awareness will exist around trauma in young asylum seekers and refugees. However, now is the time to make good decisions based on these economic forecasts by getting treatment underway as soon as it's needed in order to address adverse childhood trauma and avoid long-term health issues. Local authorities, in general, spend little on investment in this area and there is an appalling lack of specialist services across the country.

As you have previously read, psychiatrists state that every UASC should be suspected of having PTSD until otherwise proven, but do not adequately recognise that these young people are primarily wrapped in a system that is under-resourced and poorly organised. Currently, very few UASC are assessed and officially diagnosed, and fewer still receive any form of talking therapy. Therefore, much of this is rhetoric unless sufficient funding becomes available to treat those affected by trauma. UASC need to be made to feel welcome, valued and human. They need investment to achieve their potential and receive help and support when it is needed, rather than waiting years to be seen.

Although many young asylum seekers and refugees initially appear happy and devoid of trauma symptoms, reference must be made to their youth and immaturity. Often, emotional problems do not arise fully until late adolescence. An example of this is when a young person is refused LTR and this affects them greatly, resulting in stress, withdrawal, quietness, depression and self-harm. Furthermore, there is a poor cultural understanding of the stigma of mental health issues in the countries where UASC come from, which impacts on how young people think about themselves, and it is known that those who do have counselling are often subjected to silent ridicule from interpreters who judge them. As a result, their emotional pain becomes even more encapsulated, coupled with feelings of guilt and shame, as if they are bad people who have done something terribly wrong.

# Introduction

Over the past decades, thousands of young asylum seekers have entered the UK. In addition to this, Coram, the Children's Legal Centre, advises there are over 120,000 children in the UK without legal status. Half of them are thought to have been born in the country. Any young asylum seeker is highly vulnerable and at risk of being exploited or mistreated if they go missing. Some UASC go missing because they are worried that they won't be granted leave to stay in the UK and will be sent back to their country of origin. Others feel unsupported in their application for asylum. Some, after making their way to the UK alone and being independent for months or even years ever since, are unaware of what it means to be 'looked after' because there isn't a children's social care equivalent in their country of origin. Therefore, they are placed in a system that is difficult for them to fathom. This chapter will look more closely at all of the asylum pitfalls – age disputes and assessments, the substantive interviews young people undertake at the Home Office and the various outcomes – and what happens to those who don't get LTR status.

# The landscape of asylum

While it is a fact that Muslim countries have taken in asylum seekers, the Gulf States have not. Turkey has taken in approximately four million and both Lebanon and Jordan have taken in less than one million each. In 2016, pressure was placed on EU countries to take in refugees following the tragic image of a drowned young Syrian boy, who washed ashore in Turkey, which made international headlines. Afterwards, it was estimated that there were nearly 100,000 children and young people displaced in France, Italy and Greece. Public opinion forced the Conservative government of the day to act – especially after several other boats capsized in the Mediterranean.

Getting to the UK is harder than other European countries because of its geographical location, and sometimes it is said that Britain is one of the hardest places for people to be granted asylum in Western Europe – worse than Germany, France and Spain, but better than Italy. Both Greece and Italy are considered unwelcoming places for asylum-seeking young people, who are often targeted by police and subjected to aggressive interrogations. The situation is similar in Poland. Hungary is estimated to be one of the worst countries for taking in refugees, with a preference towards those who are white and Christian rather than Muslims.

Compared to countries like Libya, where murder, rape and violence are commonplace for young people and where criminals exploit them and they have to live in camps, the UK is brilliant. Young asylum seekers in France have endured heavy beatings from the police, and in Paris, where young male asylum seekers often have to sleep rough, the sights are also harrowing. Migrant families and young children in northern France are regularly evicted since the dismantling of the so-called 'Jungle' – a refugee camp where 10,000 migrants lived until 2016. Finland and Iceland have a very good reputation for their treatment of young asylum seekers, but they only take in small numbers. Belgium has a policy that places under 18s in hostels. They also have strict policies around employment (three months to get a job or else they are asked to leave).

Whether Britain shines or pales in comparison to other European countries, what isn't always recognised is the compassionate stance that many UK volunteers have taken towards helping asylum seekers and refugees on the international platform. The UK, as a whole, has not responded to various humanitarian crises across the globe. It hasn't opened up its heart to help more vulnerable children and young people. Some even say it has done the bare minimum. Compare with Germany, for example, who took in nearly a million people and offered so much help with accommodation, education and training that they became the moral lead in Europe. Sweden, too, showed great compassion and took in 60–70,000. However, it must be noted that hundreds of young volunteers from the UK have travelled to countries such as France, Turkey, Greece and others, where they have spent up to two years looking after young and vulnerable people. They have done so simply out of compassion for fellow human beings. They don't go to see. They go to help. More accolades should be given to their work.

# Breaking down barriers

Large proportions of young people make their initial claim at the airport or docks. It is estimated that approximately 6000 children arrive with their families in the UK each year. Those claiming asylum do so because of their appalling situations. Smugglers run profitable businesses – many are dangerous criminals who prey on the vulnerable and the desperate. Young people often lose their identity after they leave their home country, where they were often (or their family was) of high standing – now, nobody knows them. They are seen just as asylum seekers or refugees – their sense of identity has gone. Some young people travel from country to country seeking a secure sanctuary, presenting as 'lone rangers' seeking friendship, food and shelter in a world that often appears volatile, distrusting and unsafe. Although many come from good backgrounds in their home countries, they often have to live feral lifestyles to survive their journey to the UK. They face daily difficulties and challenges that impact greatly on their physical and emotional health as they navigate their way through uncertainty, hampered by language difficulties and little money.

## Dariush (17) from Iran

*Dariush said that after he left Iran, he travelled through Turkey, Italy and Germany before eventually ending up in Sweden. He was under the control of the agents from the start of his journey until he reached Sweden. Dariush destroyed his passport when he reached Turkey because the agent told him to do so in case he was searched and his identity was revealed. He feared this might prompt the authorities to return him home to Iran. Dariush stayed in Sweden for six months where he claimed asylum, but he felt sad most of the time and didn't care if Sweden granted him asylum because he found the place to be very racist. He said there were 12 other asylum seekers living in the same village as himself. Dariush added that the local people hated them and would always look at them with angry faces and shout, telling them they were Arabs who would ruin their country. Dariush was glad to leave Sweden because he felt so unhappy and unwelcome there. He feels safe in Britain and wants to build his future here.*

# Human rights versus hostile environment

Consecutive UK prime ministers have attempted to make the country a hostile environment for asylum seekers. Insensitive comments have ranged from describing asylum seekers as '*swarms of people coming across the Mediterranean*' to those seeking asylum as '*illegal migrants*' before adding that if somebody illegally enters the UK, the law should be enforced. The numbers allowed into the UK under resettlement programmes are also very low. Take the Syrian crisis, for example. The UK government did not do as much as it should and could have done. Their assistance was requested, but they chose not to respond. As a society, they let our fear get in the way of our humanity and they did not put human rights first. Britain did as little as possible – the bare minimum. They left the work to other countries, mainly Germany, Greece and Turkey. They initially agreed to take 3000 people, but in the end only took approximately 300. They made promises, but didn't fulfil them.

The rights of refugees and asylum seekers are protected by international law, regardless of how and why they arrive in a country. They have the same rights as everyone else, plus special or specific protections – including those outlined in the 1948 Universal Declaration of Human Rights (Article 14), which states that everyone has the right to seek and enjoy asylum from persecution in other countries. Then there is the 1951 UN Refugee Convention (and its 1967 Protocol), which states that those seeking asylum from circumstances threatening their lives or freedom cannot be penalised as illegal migrants – because under international law it dictates that they have every right to claim asylum in the UK. This is further supported by Article 3 of the European Convention on Human Rights (ECHR), which states: *'If support was refused or withdrawn would the young person be subject to treatment amounting to torture or to inhumane or degrading treatment or punishment?'*, and Article 8 of the ECHR, which states: *'If an individual returned to a country of origin, would the right for private and family life be compromised?'*

The Human Rights Act 1998 came into full effect in the UK on 2 October 2000, which meant that for first time most of the rights in the ECHR were directly enforceable in the UK. Then there is Section 55 of the Borders, Citizenship and Immigration Act 2009, which requires the Border Agency and Home Office to carry out its role in a way that takes into account the need to safeguard and promote the welfare of asylum-seeking children in the UK. Nevertheless, despite these valuable human rights laws being in place, they are side-lined by articles contained in the UK Immigration Act 2016, which gives permission to create a hostile environment for asylum seekers at every available opportunity. There are two points in the Act that particularly reinforce this.

> » The Act makes it possible for somebody to be removed after they have reached ARE but before they have had their Human Rights Assessment completed.

> » The Act also makes it illegal for somebody to rent property to anybody who has been refused LTR, as well as allowing eviction to those without status, freezing bank accounts, making it a criminal offence to work or drive, and removing leaving care support for young people whose asylum claims have failed.

Young people have built up resilience and this is sometimes as a result of how they arrived here (hazardous Channel crossings). Many cope better because they have to – sense of survival over everything else – but this isn't necessarily a skill that should be envied because they are young people who have been put through traumatic experiences well beyond their years. They have had to grow up and mature quickly. Some also know that their parents paid money for the life they have now in the UK – but the parental choice was either risk your child getting killed or send them away overseas (parental sacrifice). Many have lost parents in war zones or through ISIS or the Taliban – or they are in detention – or know they are indefinitely separated from them. They've also been separated from their country of origin, family home, friends and familiar surroundings. They have lost their sense of belonging. They question where they belong now. Many feel they have little choice in life.

# Age disputes and assessments

Upon entering the UK, each person is asked their age by Home Office representatives. If the young person self-reports to be under the age of 18, it is up to the Home Office representatives whether to believe them. Most are believed because if a 'child' is placed in detention in an adult centre for more than 24 hours, the young person can later sue the Home Office for compensation if it is proven they were illegally incarcerated. In fact, the Home Office will only treat an age-disputed child as an adult for the purposes of asylum where the applicant's physical appearance/demeanour very strongly suggests that they are *significantly* over the age of 18.

In 2014, the Department of Education (2014, p 13) outlined in a document they published about the care of unaccompanied and trafficked children that: '*Age assessments should only be carried out where there is significant reason to doubt that the claimant is a child. Age assessments should not be a routine part of a local authority's assessment of unaccompanied or trafficked children.*' However, more often than not, an age dispute and subsequent assessment intended to ascertain a '*more accurate age*' does not come until later in the asylum process. At this point, the young person may have a foster placement or be living in shared independent accommodation. They may be attending school or college and then – just as they are settling into life in Britain – something triggers a doubt within the local authority that they aren't being truthful about their age and they are, in fact, over 18.

Birth registration services are often non-functioning in the countries where young asylum seekers originate from and those who are trafficked may have been provided with documents by their traffickers. These documents can be false or genuine. They may not belong to the child or young person in question, and this casts doubt on their honesty.

The scientific basis for age assessments is controversial, since it is difficult to prove (without specific medical examinations) whether the young person is outside of the natural variation of those aged between 15 and 21. In the absence of physical tests, bone density tests and dental checks for molars, age assessments are easily the most contentious assessments carried out on asylum seekers. The outcomes can be life changing and often have profound and detrimental effects, meaning those assessed over 18 are no longer LAC. Some are wrongly assessed as adults, leaving them to navigate the system alone (more about this later).

Age assessments are sometimes carried out after adverse findings are brought to the attention of the local authority. An age assessment must follow the Merton principles (benefit of the doubt is allowed in the absence of definite evidence) and is carried out by two qualified social workers. Prior to the assessment taking place, the assessors must contact the key people involved with the young person, including teachers, foster carers, key workers and other professionals who have personally observed the young person's interaction with his/her peers. Details about the young person's background and story are put together and then, based on the balance of probability and mainly owing to general appearance and maturing demeanour, a decision is made to carry out an assessment. There are usually two physical indicators considered: the first is the general growth of the young person – their height, body build and weight; and the second is the third molar, a characteristic of adulthood rather than adolescence (but this is not definitive). Other physical factors considered include facial features (like facial hair, skin lines or folds, tone and weathering) and the young person's voice (including tone, pitch and expression), particularly in respect of males (Home Office, 2019).

If there are physical doubts, then the young person's mental maturity and demeanour are also considered. During the actual assessment, usually done over the course of three interviews, the social workers look for discrepancies in the young person's story. It is thought that a young person who has experienced an event will be able to recount central elements of the story in a broadly consistent manner and won't be evasive. They will be asked about their journey, where the assessors will look for inconsistencies in the story when checking facts about parents, siblings, culture, religion and the composition, ages, education and occupations of their family. After the story is completed, the assessors will have to determine if a reasonably consistent factual account was given and/or if any initial apparent inconsistency between the claimed age and the claimed date of birth was satisfactorily explained. Any inconsistency and remaining concerns are then presented to the young person, who is allowed to answer any doubts. An age assessment cannot be concluded with 100 per cent accuracy, owing to absent documentary evidence. With regard to discrepancies in stories, a delay in disclosing facts is not necessarily manipulative or untrue given that some trafficked young people have been given stories by their smugglers that they feel they have to keep to. A young person's account may also be affected by the impact of trauma and PTSD.

Currently, it is ad hoc as to who is chosen for assessment. Those selected have had doubts cast about them looking older than their age states or showing behavioural indicators. However, some professionals believe that every young person under the age of 18 should have an age assessment to ensure proper safeguarding measures are in place that confirm that those over the age of 18 who pose as a child are not allowed access to other children. This might, however, be seen as hypocrisy given that local authorities often have no hesitancy in mixing 16- and 17-year-olds along with young adults in shared accommodation placements in order to save money.

Out of an average of 4000 UASC annual asylum applicants, approximately 1000 applicants per annum have their age disputed. Approximately 65 per cent of these are 'found' to be over 18, despite claiming to be a child when initially applying for asylum. Many charities working with asylum seekers and refugees believe that these assessments are carried out because it suits the agenda of the local authority (ie an initiative to save money). However, more are being challenged. A UK national charity – Together with Migrant Children – is working at the forefront of this and is willing to challenge local authorities because they believe, based on the young people they work with, that over 90 per cent of negative age assessments are challengeable. The charity accepts referrals from colleges, legal centres, the British Red Cross and Coram Children's Services. They have noticed unfairness, bad practice, uncaring attitudes and even examples of when foster carers were not allowed to be part of the process. But the main prevailing issue is the lack of definite evidence that categorically proves that the young people in question are lying about their ages. Afghan boys between the ages of 15 and 17 seem to be particularly targeted by local authorities – it is the norm in their culture to age faster than western children, particularly boys who develop facial hair upon puberty.

During research for this book, Together with Migrant Children told me a story about an Afghan boy who had a passport but was still assessed as an adult. While the local authority acknowledged that the passport wasn't forged, the fact that there were date inconsistencies in some parts of his story, together with reports from professionals who considered him to be older, sealed his fate and resulted in him being considered an adult. As a result, the boy lost his accommodation and at one point slept in a park for a few nights before Together with Migrant Children was able to help him get temporary accommodation until his case could be judicially reviewed, and which the boy eventually won.

I was told that this story is not unique and it happens to many young people who are placed in hostile positions – with an unfairness existing in a system that should be protecting them. This, of course, may change in the future now that many negative age assessments are challenged – costing the local authority between £20,000 and £100,000 when it is proven that a young person was wrongly assessed as an adult. Those who are age assessed are safeguarded by the child asylum process until the local authority completes its age assessment (usually within a month), but this ultimately provides little comfort to those who receive a negative outcome.

It has to be questioned why age assessment interviews are not more legally structured, with legal representatives present for some or all of the interview process. Some other professionals I spoke to questioned why local authorities invest so much time and energy into age assessments when sometimes there is only a minor disparity in assuming somebody's correct age – for example, if somebody states they are 16 and it is suspected they might actually be 17 or 18 years old. Given that services for care leavers (or those arriving in the UK as young adults) are limited, some wonder if, for the sake of the country and the young people, it would be more compassionate to give them the benefit of the doubt. Many speak little English, are traumatised, and barely able to navigate their way in a new country, so this could give them the best possible chance of thriving in the UK instead of enduring a constant uphill struggle and being condemned to an underclass way of life. This broadens the debate on exactly what level of support young asylum seekers and refugees should be given after their eighteenth birthday when a large percentage of them struggle to cope – linguistically, culturally and mentally – irrespective of whether their claim for asylum is accepted or not.

# A failing system

Professionals who have experience of dealing with the Home Office view it as a 'massive empire' that is full of civil servants who see asylum seekers as customers first and human beings second. Some claim these officials know little about human rights and struggle to promote the welfare of the young people or act in their best interests. They have low expertise and knowledge of the issues faced by UASC. They don't care about lives being put on hold. There are totally inconsistent and implausible timeframes, especially around arranging substantive interviews, followed by long delays in making decisions. There is no consideration given to the impact this has on young people who need a system that can process a significant event in their lives as expediently as possible. Yet, the backlog of applications waiting to be processed is deemed unacceptably high by professionals in the field, adding that the lengthy delays incur further reputational damage to the Home Office.

Hardly any investment in trauma-informed practice is provided, despite emphasis on this in the community among professionals working with young people. At the moment, there is little consideration given to trauma and how a lengthy wait for a Home Office decision can heighten this. There are also accounts of 'aging out' applicants, because after they reach 18 the young people are interviewed as adults. They lose protection because their case is no longer viewed as that of a child, even though they may have applied for asylum when they were well under 18. Therefore, young asylum seekers need to be screened much faster than at present. The system needs to be clearer. Young people need to know where they stand much sooner – ideally before they reach 18. It is claimed that the Home Office is full of pockets of poor practices. Caseworkers don't receive adequate training for their roles. There is a high staff turnover, often entailing demoralised staff who are unable to cope with heavy caseloads. The structure is highly dysfunctional in the sense that there is no regulation of staff or their work, which means cases can be forgotten about or left in transit without any consequences.

What is the true narrative? Does political motivation depend on which political party is in government? It could also be a case of different leaders and ministers within the same party implementing different polices. Many question if there is a hidden political agenda and why the whole system is woefully slow (often for no apparent reason other than it is meant to demonstrate how difficult it is to get asylum in the UK – after all, if the Home Office is viewed as being too generous, will others follow?).

Promises of a new system that better serves the interests of applicants have been ongoing for years. Failed promises of devising a framework that will keep to timescales is commonplace. Targets have not been met in years. The current timescale between substantive interviews and young people receiving their decisions is set at six months. Few are received within this timescale. This means that once the timescale is exceeded, concentration is prioritised on the cases that are still under six months in order to meet targets. However, poor performance management is still highly visible, even in this latter initiative. The system is thoroughly flawed and dysfunctional.

Young people need opportunities to move on with their lives. Their futures cannot be put on hold. But under the current framework, life for the majority means waiting in limbo, including not being allowed to work. Solicitors are also often found to be slow or unwilling to either approach the Home Office over lengthy waits for decisions or address failed timescales, despite them not receiving any funds under legal aid until the applicant has been granted LTR status.

# Substantive interviews

Young people who arrive and claim asylum in the UK initially undertake a Home Office welfare screening interview before being asked to complete their Statement of Evidence Form (SEF). This form outlines the prime reason why they are applying for asylum in the UK. Once the SEF has been submitted, the young person must wait to be called to their substantive interview at the Home Office.

In most cases, either a social worker (for those under 18) or a personal adviser (for those over 18) will attend substantive interviews with young asylum seekers. Their main role is to act as a responsible adult and ensure everything is in place to promote equality and fairness during the interview. They are also there to offer moral support and reassurance to the young person and ensure everything is explained to them. This includes making sure the young person's legal representative is present and that the young person has had adequate preparation time with them before their interview. As a social worker, I have assisted many young people to prepare and attend their substantive interviews. I have made sure they have seen their solicitor prior to the interview and then accompanied them to Lunar House in East Croydon where the Home Office conducts most of their asylum interviews. The young people I supported were often tense and nervous and required moral support and reassurance. Many were so anxious that they were unable to eat breakfast, so I always ensured that I carried fruit and/or bars of chocolate in my bag to give to them in such cases.

For those under 18, Home Office interviews usually last half a day, depending on the complexity of the case. A maximum of six people are present in the interview.

1. The young person.

2. The young person's responsible adult.

3. The young person's legal representative.

4. An interpreter for the legal representative.

5. The interviewing officer.

6. A Home Office interpreter (main interpreter).

The reason for having two interpreters present is to ensure that no irregularity or miscommunication takes place in the interview between the young person, the Home Office interpreter and the interviewing officer. The interpreter from the legal team is allowed to interject if they feel something hasn't been sufficiently interpreted – or has been misinterpreted.

The responsible adult is not usually allowed to answer any questions on behalf of the young person, although sometimes the interviewing officer may ask the responsible adult if they know GP contact details or information about the college the young person is attending. The role of the responsible adult is mainly to ensure the young person is treated well and to interject (or stop the interview) if the young person gets tired, hungry, needs a comfort break or becomes emotional. They can also intervene if the young person is having difficulties with the interpreter (although this should also be picked up by the interviewing officer). Personally, I have never witnessed a young person being unfairly treated in substantive interviews, although some have become withdrawn or silent when discussing aspects of their story, particularly when speaking about their families.

There are parts of the substantive interview that I consider nonsensical, however, especially when young people are routinely asked simple questions (that never vary) about their country of origin – for example, being asked to describe the national flag, the currency and the different denominations used, as well as other easy questions about food, religious festivals and dress codes. Did it never occur to the Home Office that young people talk to each other about what is asked during their interviews or that a simple ten-minute Google search would amply provide basic information needed to answer these questions? It sometimes feels like we are living in a world of stupidity during such moments.

I have also often sat in interviews thinking how different it would be if I was the interviewer – what questions I would ask the young person rather than the usual round of going over information contained in their personal statement that never seems to yield anything new or different, given that young people rehearse their statements incessantly. This goes back to my point in Chapter 1 when I referred to 'thin' (not entirely true) and 'thick' (real) stories. In other words, parts of the true story of the young person are mingled with a story given to them by their smugglers who have convinced them that this is the best strategy to get LTR status. The young people know that if they change the details given in their initial screening interview (when they first arrive in the country) or in their statement, they will have to justify and explain the change(s). Therefore, a charade is often played out between the young person and the interviewing officer, during which the responsible adult and others in the room sit and listen.

On several occasions, I could not help but wonder what the young person's real story was and imagined taking them to another room where they would be completely free (without any penalty) to tell the full truth about their life, identity, family and background story and the circumstances that brought them to the UK. I imagine the truth would still reveal persecution, oppression, war, death, pain and suffering. One cannot help but wonder if Britain is a country unable to hear the truth, given that these young people are so desperately fearful of not being believed if they were to tell the full and factual account of their lives. So instead, we have to contend with the part truth and part fiction given to us by young people who are desperate to be given their LTR status. And it is by these methods that their fate is decided.

# Amer (17) from Iraq

*I have never known a day's happiness in my life. Can you imagine that? I'm only 17 years of age. I had good parents but growing up with war meant constantly being told 'don't go here' and 'don't go there'. Danger was never far away. I am trying to create a life for myself here in Britain, with college and work experience. But I know that everything can be taken away from me if I don't get my papers. We hear news from home that tells us the place is getting worse. The situation is not getting better. Anybody who is Iraqi knows that. But the Home Office might think it's safe for me to go to another town or city and want to send me back.*

*I have friends. I smile and I laugh, but underneath my head is exploding with worry and full of thoughts about what will or won't happen. There is no happiness in my life, not knowing what the future holds. Unless a person has peace in their soul, they can never be happy. I wake up from nightmares in the middle of the night, thinking that my friends are going to kill me. I lie awake for a while before realising this is not true. My mind might switch then to dreams of winning the lottery and buying a Lamborghini, before it wanders back to Iraq and the division in my town between Sunni and Shi'a Muslims and the threats they made against my family.*

*Do you know they inflict such torture on themselves? They even use swords to slash their backs and the top of their heads. This is for the guilt they feel for having killed the prophet's grandson. Imagine, if they do that to themselves, what they would do to me? But this could be my fate and nobody will care. They might expect me to go back and settle in a place where I'll know nobody, with no family or friends or proper home. I would never be able to find a job. Hospitals would turn me away if I was sick, because I wasn't registered with them when I was young. I would have a terrible life, one that would not be worth living.*

*When you claim asylum you become part of a system where social workers will constantly tell you that 'this will happen or that might happen or this could happen, or perhaps this might be the answer to it if this happens ...', but this all just adds to a life that is already full of uncertainty. Nobody you meet knows anything for sure. Social workers are like different types of fruit that all taste differently. Lies are often told.*

*Some days I feel like shutting myself away at home and not trying any more. Maybe this is what will happen if I don't get my papers. What would be the point in trying anymore? Maybe the only help available to me after I'm 18 and if I'm refused leave to stay is help from the British Red Cross. They might put me in a place where I would have to sleep with seven others in a room. I heard stories about this. What sort of life would that be?*

# Asylum outcomes

The following is a description of the main outcomes given to asylum claims made by young people in the UK. The ambition is to receive an initial five years, with the intention thereafter of applying for permanency and British citizenship.

## Refugee status

Refugee status is granted for five years, under the UN Refugee Convention, to a person who has a well-founded fear of persecution – namely because of their race, religion, nationality, political option or because they fall within a particular social group (the LGBT community, a victim of trafficking or the fact that they are a child). Once LTR is given, it is seldom revoked unless the young person commits a serious offence or is found to have lied in their application.

## Humanitarian protection

Humanitarian protection is granted for five years, although the applicant is refused asylum because they do not meet the criteria of the UN Refugee Convention. However, the Home Office considers it too dangerous to return them back to their country of origin because they face a real risk of serious harm – including the death penalty, unlawful killing and torture.

This is a form of immigration status. It is granted by the Home Office to a person who it decides has a need for protection because there is a serious risk that their rights, under Article 3 ECHR, would be breached or they could be unlawfully killed or face the death penalty if they returned home. As with LTR refugee status, once humanitarian protection is given, it is seldom revoked, unless the young person commits a serious offence or is found to have lied in their application.

## Limited leave as an unaccompanied asylum-seeking child

## (UASC leave)

The applicant is given limited LTR when they are refused refugee status and humanitarian protection. This is granted when the Home Office recognises that, as children, it is not possible to return them to their country of origin. Therefore, they are granted discretionary leave until they reach 17.5 years of age. When they reach this age, they must then lodge a further application to extend their stay or a fresh application for asylum. If an appeal fails, extensions of UASC leave cannot be applied for until the child is over 17.5. Extension applications must be made before the expiry of leave (or the young person becomes an overstayer).

Approximately 50 per cent of children receive temporary refugee status up to the age of 17.5 years. How do you address the future of that child? How can social workers plan for that child? Not many of the children understand the ramifications. UASC leave should be abolished because this puts young people in situations of misguided trust – 'I'll be fine – I'll get my papers' – only to be refused later.

## Discretionary leave (DL) and leave outside the rules (LOTR)

This is given when someone is refused asylum and/or humanitarian protection. Instead they are given either discretionary leave (DL) which is granted by the Home Office meaning someone can live and work in the UK for a designated period of time - or leave outside the rules (LOTR) which is given for other reasons, including: medical, victims of modern slavery and trafficking, family or private life.

## Limited Leave to Remain on family or private life grounds

Limited LTR is given to children who have lived here for many years and who would have difficulties adjusting to life abroad on family or private grounds. It is given for two and a half years before a further asylum application is made.

# Statistics

It is estimated that the following statistics apply for young people claiming asylum:

> » 58 per cent receive refugee status/humanitarian protection (enabling them to create a life in the UK that will lead to them getting permanent status);

> » 26 per cent receive UASC leave;

> » 16 per cent outright refusal.

The benefits to those who are given five-year refugee status or humanitarian protection means they are automatically assigned similar rights as permanent residents, including being able to legally work and apply for a driving licence. For those seeking further education, they qualify for home fees and are eligible for student loans if in higher education. Those with refugee status can apply for travel documents (similar to passports), or a Certificate of Travel (CoT) if granted humanitarian protection. However, applying for CoT doesn't mean they will be able to travel to countries that are party to the Schengen Agreement, including mainstream Europe (Spain, Portugal, Germany, France, Greece and Italy). Both travel permits prevent travel to the young person's country of origin.

## Outright refusal

Those whose submitted claims are refused are usually refused because they lack credibility (ie their account was insufficiently detailed or had unexplained gaps or inconsistencies) and knowledge in the interview, and the risk of persecution that would prevent relocation back to their home country was not sufficiently established. There are also times when someone's nationality is disputed – for example, Egyptians claiming to be Syrians, or Sudanese claiming to be Eritreans. However, reasons for refusal often provide little consolation for the young people who find themselves in this situation. They are the same person with the same story. They have done nothing wrong. The Home Office simply hasn't believed them.

Nobody is able to challenge the Home Office. It often has a political agenda when it comes to the facts of countries. Sometimes the situations in these countries are poorly researched and contain outdated information. People who are refused, however, receive a written outline as to why their application was declined. They must lodge an appeal within 14 days. Such appeals are heard in an asylum court under what is initially known as a 'First Tier appeal', where a judge considers all aspects of the asylum claim and makes a new decision based on the evidence at the date of appeal. If the outcome remains negative, it can then be sent to an Upper Tribunal if it is felt that the Home Office has made errors or if the negative decision had inadequate reasons for refusal. Failing that, there are two other avenues based on the evidence and strength of the case including the two other higher chambers – the Court of Appeal and the Supreme Court.

## Human Rights Assessments (HRA)

These assessments are as controversial as age dispute assessments because there is a lack of parity of esteem in how they are carried out or how the outcomes are implemented, depending on which local authority is responsible. Some local authorities do not undertake these assessments until the young person is aged 21 (or 25 if in higher education). HRAs are carried out when the 'end of the line' is reached in the appeals process and the young person is deemed to have reached the point of ARE.

Although guidelines state that it's not for the local authority to draw its open conclusions, there is little or no power that over-governs their decisions. Most HRA assessments are carried out by the local authority, with no person outside the council present. This is considered unfair, given the absence of any real scrutiny. They are often punitive and very seldom rule in the young person's favour. A negative outcome means that support will be withdrawn from the local authority, including accommodation and financial assistance. Basically, some local authorities do not want to be seen to be supporting young asylum seekers who have had unsuccessful appeals and now find themselves in the position of being deemed ARE. Most young people in this position decline Home Office support that is intended to return them to their country of origin and are likely to disappear to a large city and work illegally.

## Fresh claims

Fresh claims for asylum are submitted in person to the Home Office in Liverpool. They must contain new evidence and/or new witnesses and/or new documents that cast doubt on the original decision. This needs to be considered alongside information previously submitted in the initial claim of asylum. If the fresh claim is recognised, a young person could be granted refugee status or they may be refused with a new right of appeal – delaying the onset of ARE. However, if a new claim is not recognised as a fresh claim, it is refused with no right of appeal. The young person may then be detained and removed.

# Support for refused asylum seekers

The prospect of being sent to a deportation centre looms over the heads of young people who reach ARE. Many have no families to return to and, with no support on the horizon back home, this means significant risks. Several are not old enough to cope and nobody cares how they will manage. The other alternative to detention is Section 4 support from the Home Office. The young person will sign an agreement that they will not lodge any further appeal and will return to their country of origin. They are placed in Home Office accommodation and given a weekly financial allowance to cover food costs. However, weekly reporting to ensure monitoring of the person at the UK Visas and Immigration Agency (a division of the Home Office) is usually a condition attached to agreeing to this support.

The number of children who return to their countries (either voluntarily or forced) are really low. But for those who are refused refugee status to remain, it often means the start of a horrible life in the UK – without proper accommodation and legitimate employment. There is also a terrible sense of failure and worthlessness, including a huge psychological impact for the young people whose parents spent the last of their money on giving their child the opportunity for a better life. Young people in this situation will go to any length to ensure they find a way of lodging a fresh application for asylum. Those in limbo have little option but to seek help and support mainly from charitable organisations – unless they 'disappear' and decide to go into hiding, fearing that they will face persecution or imprisonment for reasons of race, religion, nationality or their political views if they return home.

The British Red Cross helps with voluntary returns, including having conversations with clients that they don't want to hear. They help people out of destitution by providing some financial support and making referrals to food banks. They also steer people towards a different solicitor or other legal expert who might review their cases and/or lodge a fresh asylum claim if new evidence emerges. Referrals are also made to hosting charities for those urgently in need of accommodation.

Hosting charities are made up entirely of volunteers and are funded through grants and private individuals. These charities consist of people who are willing to offer a room to an asylum seeker (over the age of 18) who was initially refused asylum and has now reached the end of the appeal process, also resulting in an unfavourable outcome. Asylum seekers like this are often in desperate need of accommodation and are at serious risk of becoming homeless and destitute. Hosting charities provide a national service throughout the UK and they fulfil a great need in supporting asylum seekers who are refused refugee status and do not receive care or statutory services.

In the cases of those in the aftercare service, once an asylum seeker reaches ARE at the end of the appeal process, a Human Rights Assessment is carried out by the 18plus team. If there are no mitigating circumstances (eg a person has a serious mental health problem), the likelihood is that support from the local authority is withdrawn based on the premise that the Home Office has deemed it safe for the applicant to return to their homeland.

Referrals to hosting charities usually come from the 18plus service or the British Red Cross, although charities do accept self-referrals. The criteria for referrals are those who have reached ARE but are in the process of making a fresh application for asylum. They need to be actively engaged in collecting evidence, and hosting charities usually request that they are linked to an agency who monitor their case, such as the British Red Cross, so they will have a named person to provide consistency for the asylum seeker.

Finding a solicitor who takes on ARE cases is difficult because cases are only accepted on merit based on the probability of winning and, providing it is realistic, that the young person can obtain the evidence needed to prove their case. Once a claim is ready to be submitted, the asylum seeker is given an appointment to attend the Further Submissions Unit in Liverpool, but there is sometimes a waiting list of between three and four months to be seen. How is a destitute person expected to find funds to travel to Liverpool other than via a charity? Once a fresh claim is accepted and being processed, it usually takes between 12 and 18 months to process, although in certain cases it has been known to take years. In the meantime, the person's life is in limbo. They have nowhere to live, no recourse to benefits and they are also forbidden to work. The psychological impact this has on an individual is sometimes overwhelming and they can lapse into periods of depression and anxiety.

Accommodation is usually given in the community where the asylum seeker has previously lived, near to their legal advisers, mental health support and the local mosque or church they have been attending. In accommodation settings, asylum seekers are known as 'guests' and the provider as 'hosts'. Hosts tend to be aged 40-plus and come mainly from middle-class or middle-upper-class backgrounds. An assessment is carried out with each host and, while there is no formal training, the charities offer guidance on how PTSD manifests itself in order to help them spot the signs and symptoms to report to their link worker. There are some basic rules around times for bathroom usage and keeping their room clean and tidy. Other difficulties may arise if, say, a host is vegetarian and the guest eats meat, until a compromise is reached. Hosts are advised against giving advice to guests about their respective cases.

Hosts offer a room in their homes for a set period – which can be a week, month or longer. Some offer indefinitely. It is usually expected that the hosts offer the guests at least one hot meal daily, although some hosts provide full board. Hosting charities usually pay a bursary of £20 a week to each person. Their other services include making referrals to food banks or directing people to free courses and community groups, where they can cook together. Some are encouraged to become volunteers. They may also attend support groups for people suffering from depression and anxiety (referrals are made through the British Red Cross). Long-term friendships and lasting bonds are formed, and it is not uncommon for guests to refer fondly to their host and the host's family as their family too, and vice versa.

Hosting charities usually do not offer accommodation to asylum seekers who have reached the point of ARE for a second time – ie their second claim has been refused and the appeals process has been exhausted. In cases like this, the person can end up being placed in a removal detention centre or housed in Section 4 Accommodation under the National Asylum Support Service (NASS). Here they often live in cramped and substandard conditions until they are called for deportation. Many refuse to live in such conditions, where they are offered just over £35 a week for food, and it is mainly at this point when somebody has lost all hope of ever living legally in Britain that they decide to go 'underground' – they disappear into the community with only a few people, if any, knowing their whereabouts.

Accommodation in London, especially those who submit a second time, is still favoured and many ask hosting charities if they can be placed there. Asylum seekers believe that if they are given refugee status, then because they already know London well at that stage and have developed roots there, it will be easier to find a job. Another important task carried out by hosting charities is the help they offer those living in Section 4 accommodation (who came to the UK as adults) who get refugee status but are given 28 days to vacate their accommodation. Often this short notice period is not enough time for refugees to get re-housed through lack of funding and unemployment and once again they have little choice but to reach out to charitable organisations for help.

# Legal aid

The general consensus among many professionals working with asylum seekers is that there are few good solicitors and even fewer outstanding ones. The quality of legal aid in the UK for asylum seekers generally consists of poor practice, poor training and poor knowledge of the appeals process. This projects the overall impression that the system is poorly supervised in this area. The system seems to work better with initial claims, but lacks prowess in dealing with appeals – although insufficient funding is a contributing factor here. It is often seen as a profit-making business consisting of some solicitors having a low understanding of the cases they are presenting and/or the personal experiences their clients have gone through to get to the UK. They also often lack knowledge and expertise in mental health matters, child sexual exploitation and the sexual abuse encountered en route to the UK. Others have little knowledge of the types of report they should request from the Home Office in relation to a young person's individual needs (ie CAMHS or a report outlining special needs).

It is felt there needs to be greater investment in legal aid and in more trained solicitors who better understand the system, as well as an increase in specialists who have a better understanding of young people. Social workers also need to have a better grasp of the legal system, including knowing what is the best and most appropriate support to ensure a young person is given correct information and fully understands the legal process. Broadly speaking, while not expecting social workers to be immigration experts, they need to have enough understanding of the system to ask questions and to know what legal questions to ask on behalf of the child.

Social workers, immigration lawyers and the police do not share information or expertise. At the moment, these services are not connected and often the right hand does not consult with the left. However, this is not an isolated problem within the arena of asylum-seeking young people, but what it does highlight is the lack of importance attached to delivering services to young people under local authorities. What isn't often realised within Children's Services is that if the UK gets it right for young asylum seekers and refugees, then they will get it right for citizen children as well.

# Survivors

Despite some young people having a bad start, especially when things haven't worked out as well as planned, they nevertheless overcome obstacles mainly as a result of professionals (social workers, foster carers and 18plus personal advisers) who are willing to go beyond what is expected of their position. It is these young people who do exceptionally well in their life choices of college, career and relationships. It is because of these brave and wonderful individuals in the system who help this happen, as opposed to the system itself, which is often described as being developed to do the bare minimum. But what about those who do not receive their LTR status or are at risk of becoming ARE in the appeal process?

Solutions are needed for young people who are at the end of the line with their asylum claims. They need professionals who know the system and have a good level of understanding of the options available to those who are and have very few choices. For those who have no status, what do they do? For those with criminal convictions, what do they do? For those who are threatened with return, what do they do?

Local authorities have borne the brunt of responsibility for young asylum seekers, despite insufficient funding from the Home Office. Nevertheless, services across the country vary from the good to the not so good. But can you entirely blame local authorities at a time when government funding is so low? When they struggle to deliver an 'optimum' service for all children? There are several good pieces of practice that go unnoticed, including helping young asylum seekers who are suicidal and those requiring differing levels of support because of their vulnerability.

## Triple planning

It is important for social workers and 18plus personal advisers to liaise closely with each other prior to the young person's eighteenth birthday and handover to the leaving care service. A triple planning meeting needs to take place, where the three possible outcomes are explained to the young people who are still waiting for the outcome of their asylum application.

The following factors need to be taken into consideration.

» Equipping young people with the best possible life in the UK until they receive the outcome of their asylum application.

» Supporting young people who are going through the appeal process – or when they have exhausted all appeals but are not removed.

» Preparing young people to be returned to their country of origin if they are refused and lose subsequent appeals – or if they decide to return of their own accord (extremely few choose this option).

Sometimes young people are prepared for the transition to the 18plus team, which effectively sees them being treated as care leavers and young adults. For those who have lived in the UK for several years, there is little difficulty in their transition – especially if they have refugee status and speak good English. However, for those who may only have been in the UK for six months and are still awaiting their substantive interview and speak little English, it will prove far more difficult. These young people may already be struggling with understanding their Child in Need status and having a social worker, and then suddenly this switches to a completely different department with an 18plus personal adviser who will expect them to be more independent and self-sufficient than what was previously expected of them. Often, the different services and professionals become confusing for some young people who are unable to differentiate between them, despite the endeavours of professionals preparing them for this transition. I will return to this later in the chapter on young adults, Chapter 8.

# Conclusion

Britain is the sixth richest country in the world, yet still has a system that struggles to help young asylum seekers whose lives, through no fault of their own, have been blighted by huge personal difficulties and loss from a young age. Of course, some may argue that they get a good service and are well treated in comparison to how their home countries treated them. But this is hardly a correct and meaningful response. Professionals interviewed for this book have told me, time and time again, about poor services and practices here in the UK mingled with uncompassionate attitudes and ineptitude. Improvements to services are needed to help those new to the UK who struggle to find their way and fit in. But sadly, it is perhaps too late for many young people over the age of 18 who have had to bear the brunt of an often-unhelpful system that failed to help and protect them as they deserved.

Life is really tough for young asylum seekers and refugees – even for those with LTR status – because, in addition to having to deal with all of the emotional angst that comes with adolescence and young adulthood, these young people often do so without the direct support of parents and family. So, in addition to dealing with these stresses, they also endure the emotional turmoil of having to constantly worry about their long-term security and well-being. Making comparisons to other young people is inevitable – the feeling of not wanting to be the one who fails is ever present, along with an endless plethora of confusion and injustices and the continuous anxiety that exists in this arena of daily living.

# Introduction

In writing this book, I wanted to include as many 'voices' of young people as possible. Teaching creative writing to a group of ESOL students at London South East College in Plumstead provided me with an excellent opportunity. Here, young people – both male and female, and from Vietnam, Eritrea, Sudan and Somalia – kindly agreed to participate in my lessons knowing that their writings would be published in this book. During the lessons, I introduced topics I felt were relevant to the lives of young refugees and asylum seekers – which would enable them to improve their emotional literacy and become better at describing their feelings. Before the students were asked to write their stories, a group discussion about the chosen topic always took place at the start of the lesson. This enabled the students, who were often enthusiastic and engaging, to become better equipped at shaping their thoughts before then expressing them on paper. The results, as you will see, are often insightful, reflective and sometimes amusing.

# The beginning

Exploring how well they settled into this country and their new environments, this exercise consisted of six questions getting the young people to reflect on their initial experiences of when they first arrived in the UK.

> » What did you miss most about home after you left your country?
>
> » What were your first impressions of Britain on the first day you arrived?
>
> » Who was helpful to you when you first arrived?
>
> » What did you fear most when you first arrived in Britain?
>
> » Do you have any funny stories to tell about your first few weeks here?
>
> » What was your worst experience during those first few weeks?

## Aziz from Eritrea

*Actually, what I miss a lot about my homeland is so many things, but mostly my family. My family is everything to me and we used to do many things together – playing, cooking and sharing love. What I mean by that is when one of my family gets hurt or feels down, my mum used to motivate us to get better. My first impression coming to the UK was arriving safe and healthy. The second one was noticing its attractive buildings. I find the UK much better than the other countries I was in before coming here. What I mean by that is it is better than Switzerland. I was there for three years before they kicked me out. Here I am treated well. When I arrived in the UK, the police were very kind to me. When I asked them to help me, they were so positive. This was good because, after I arrived, I was frightened about where the authorities would take me to live and if I would be safe. The immigration office, what I want to say about that is they took a lot of time to tell me about my asylum – all of my friends have got their positive permit, but I am still waiting for an answer from the Home Office. That's my worst experience.*

## Dung from Vietnam

*My name is Dung. I am Vietnamese. I have been in London now for a year. I really missed my family after I left home. There were many things that impressed me when I first arrived, but the first thing was the weather. The weather in London is really cold in the winter and I still cannot get used to it now. I was so frightened of my ability to survive, mainly because I had so little money. I wondered if I would starve to death. But after a few weeks, my social worker helped me sort everything out. My solicitor was also helpful. I found it strange living in a house without my family, but my foster family were good to me – although with little English I used to have to use body language to speak to them. At first, I did not leave the house often because I was shy of going into shops by myself. I could not answer them when it came to paying. I'll never forget those experiences. But now, I can live without that fear and I hope I can have a good life in the UK.*

## Guhaad from Somalia

*I used to live in Sweden for five years before moving to London. I must say I miss my family most of all, but I was so excited to come to Britain because I had reached my goal by coming here. I felt lonely at first because I didn't have any friends, but now I have made many friends. Thankfully, I haven't had any bad experiences since coming here. My social worker and key worker have helped me. I remember something funny when I first arrived. I was sitting in Starbucks one day and I kept watching the coffee machines and how they worked! We don't have machines like that in Somalia.*

## Cam from Vietnam

*I've been in England now for 11 months. After I left home, I missed my friends and food in Vietnam. When I came to England, I felt it was a modern country with many high buildings and many cars. I'm excited with the weather. It's cooler than Vietnam. I like people in England. They're very friendly and kind. I felt very lucky because, after I arrived, I met a Vietnamese lady. She took care of me for a few days – and then she took me to the solicitors. I was really worried and scared about what will happen to me in the future. At the time, I wasn't able to speak much English and had no money. I asked myself what I should do as I didn't have anything. But I managed, especially after I went to live with my foster carer. At first, we used to use Google Translate to talk to each other because some of the words I said, she didn't understand, or I used bad words – wrong meaning by accident, which made her laugh! Now, I'm very happy living in the UK. I am going to college and learning English. I love the family I am living with because they are very kind to me.*

## Faheen from Sudan

*When I left my country, I missed my family and friends because they are the most important things in my life. The police got me and took me to the police station, where they put me in their jail for 12 hours because there wasn't any place for me to stay overnight. The next day, in the morning, they took me back to a foster carer's house. At first, I liked the UK and was surprised to meet people from many different countries, but there have been times when I hated it – mainly because I wasn't able to understand or communicate with people. One day, I went into the ladies' toilet by mistake! The worst thing about coming here was the thought that I would never see my family again and that I would never be able make friends.*

## Rada from Vietnam

*I think I missed everything after I left my home country, especially my family. Sometimes I missed the weather because my country just has two seasons – wet and dry. On my first day here, I was very excited because the weather was very warm and sunny and the sky was very blue. Everyone was friendly, helpful and kind – although my English was not good at first, people still helped me whenever I asked them for help with my problems. At first, I could not understand what people were saying because they spoke very fast and their accents were difficult to hear. In the first few weeks, I didn't know how to use the underground because there are so many different lines. I was stuck in a station for over an hour trying to figure out the right direction. My worst experience was when one day somebody stole my purse when I was out walking on the street. Although I didn't have much money in it, that was my favourite purse.*

## Jamal from Sudan

*Every day I miss everyone and everything. I left my country when I was 12 years old. I miss my family, friends and country – everything. But I was hopeful that I had come to a safe country. I was shocked because I didn't think all the houses on my street would all look the same. I was also frightened of having to go to school. I woke up the first day crying, but after that things got better – although I was confused when I had to speak English at school. The people are friendly, but the weather is the worst thing. You need a jacket nearly all of the year or else you are freezing.*

## Hau from Vietnam

*My name is Hau and I am from Vietnam. I've been in England for nearly two years. I came to England by plane. I still remember arriving here. I didn't know anything. Everything was very strange to me because this was my first time to be in a new country. I didn't have any family here and I didn't know how to speak English. I went to a temple so that I could meet other Vietnamese people to help me. I stayed in the temple for three days before somebody took me to a solicitor where I asked for help with asylum. After that I was taken to meet my social worker. She took me to meet my foster family. Everybody was so kind to me. I really like going to college and have made many new friends.*

# Relationships

Looking towards the future and exploring love and commitment was part of this exercise. Many of the young people in the group were devout Muslims or Christians and did not believe in sex before marriage. Everybody in the group, though, was able to envisage their ideal life after they had completed their education and were in stable employment. The question:

*Imagine you are 25+ years of age, you have permanent residency, finished college and have qualifications. You also have a good job. Now, it's time to get married. What type of person would you like to marry or be in a relationship with? What sort of qualities do you like in a boyfriend/ girlfriend – caring, intelligent, good looking? What type of house would you like to live in? Do you want to have children?*

## Dung from Vietnam

*After I have finished college and have qualifications, I need to think about my own family. I would like to have a nice girlfriend. I don't mind so much where my girlfriend is from – I just would like to have a kind girl, somebody who is intelligent. I hope she can look after my family really well. I would like to see a peaceful atmosphere when I come back home from work. About the house we live in, I don't want to live in noisy places. I would like a quiet house because my job might make me stressed enough. And I would like to live near my parents' house. Then if they have something wrong, I can come quickly and help them. About the children, I don't want to have children too early. I would like to think about that one year after I get married. And I don't want to have too many children, just two is enough. I'll be busy if I have too many. I hope I have enough free time for my family. That's my dream about a nice future.*

## Jamal from Sudan

*Before I get married, I would like to be with my girlfriend for five years and then it would be time for us to get married. Nowadays, most people would love to be in a relationship with a good-looking person before they see the true personality of the person and then they break up – but I am different from these kinds of people. I always look at the personality first, so if you go with personality you will get to know your girlfriend better before you get married – so you never lose.*

## Cartan from Somalia

*At the time I've finished college and got a good job, I'll start the relationship route in love. I would like to be in a relationship with somebody who is caring, good behaviour and not thinking about just themselves, but also to think about me as well – and, yes, I would like to be in a relationship with somebody who is good looking and has a beautiful face. She has to be intelligent, kind and smart. I want a person who respects me and my opinions, even when it is different to theirs. I would like to feel safe when I'm with her because I want to be comfortable. I'll be proud if I get my dream relationship. I'm looking forward to getting the best relationship. We will allow each other space. I would like to save money, and for me and my girlfriend to trust each other with money. After we get married, we can have the same bank account provided we trust each other.*

## Hau from Vietnam

*When I get older and have finished college and have a good job, I want to marry somebody who is independent, intelligent and especially somebody who loves me. I think the characteristics are more important than the appearance, however, I prefer somebody who is taller than me. I would love to be in a relationship with a good-looking person, not really handsome but nice looking. I will choose someone who knows how to cook rather than someone who has another talent. After that, we will live in a house with a big yard and a rose garden, and a big kitchen full of appliances because I really like cooking. I want to have two children. It will be good if I have one boy and one girl. I hope that when I get older, I will meet some-body like I've described and that we will have a happy life together.*

## Biniam from Eritrea

*The girl that I'd like to spend my whole life with should have good qualities. What I mean is a good personality like self-independence, caring, brave, good manners, respectful and humorous. Actually, I am a person who doesn't care that much about appearance because I prefer inner beauty. Outside appearance changes over time; however, inner beauty never gets old. The reason most people get divorced is because they didn't get to know each other very well beforehand, or they hide their behaviour. They appeared good on the outside, however, after they discovered their true behaviour, it is then they get hurt. My point is you have to take time to get to know a person – you shouldn't hurry to marry. I'm sure one day I'll find my soulmate.*

## Cam from Vietnam

*I don't have a boyfriend now, but I still hope to be settled when I am 27 years old. That is after I have a good job and have travelled some countries with my friends. I don't really need a rich man, but I wish him to be good, intelligent and a hard-working man. He can also cook me some nice food. In the future, I can buy a house. I want to decorate my home with bright colours and have nice furniture. I also want to have a garden where I can plant flowers and vegetables. I want to have children after I get married. I want to enjoy my life with my husband.*

## Demsas from Eritrea

*I just want to marry a kind and beautiful person. I need to get married – not for my sake, of course, but for my family and for society to accept me. I just want to have children and a big house, big enough for my family.*

# Identity, culture, religion and integration

This exercise consisted of a series of questions that asked the young people to explore diversity and inclusion, enabling them to think about the views and opinions of others that are different to themselves.

» What does your religion mean to you?

» Do you think there is a difference between religion and culture?

» Do you respect that Britain is a Christian country – and why?

» If you are a Muslim – have you ever been inside a church? If you are Christian – have you ever been inside a mosque? What about other places of worship?

» How many of you are friends with somebody different to yourself – eg a white English person, a gay person, or somebody with a disability?

» Do you think all people are equal – or not?

## Aaden from Eritrea

*At the moment, I call myself black Eritrean, but maybe in the future – if I get my papers – I will call myself black British. The most important thing for refugees to integrate in Britain is the freedom to communicate to people from other countries. You can walk wherever you want so there is no problem talking to different types of people. Religion is the most important thing in my life – and I can't live without God. Religion, though, is talking about God, but culture is different. Culture means talking about people living in the same country and practising the same customs and having the same values. I respect Britain, but I don't like seeing gay people kissing in public. I was in a cafe recently and saw two men sitting next to me kissing. I don't think this should be allowed in Britain. I know that most British people come from a Christian background. I am Muslim and am able to practise my religion here. I go to the mosque whenever I can, but mainly on Fridays. I believe everybody on earth is equal, whatever their religion or background.*

## Mohamed from Sudan

*The purpose of religion is to ensure that people can live in harmony together, to tell the truth, be honest and honourable to people, but religion is a way of creating order. Anybody can make a small group of people live under the same rules, but you need something like religion to make sure everybody behaves themselves. If people believe that God is watching over them, they won't do bad things like stealing, getting in fights, drinking alcohol or committing rape. In China, they believe in Buddhism; in Europe, they believe in Christianity; and in the Middle East, they have Islam. Everybody thinks that their religion is the correct one. I am Muslim. When I was young, I asked my parents why they thought that Islam was the correct religion to follow. They told me that Islam was the last and most developed religion in the world and that it was getting more followers day by day, and that was how they knew it is the correct religion.*

## Rada from Vietnam

*I'm Vietnamese and I'm an asylum seeker. I feel safe in the UK. It is important for young asylum seekers to make friends with people from other countries. Religion means to me Buddhism, because the majority of Vietnamese follow Buddhism as that is the main religion in our country. I don't practise my religion on a regular basis, but I do sometimes go to the temple with my friends – but I have also visited Christian churches. I respect that Britain is a Christian country. Although most of my friends are Vietnamese, when I go to college, I am able to meet and talk to other friends from different countries.*

## Hanad from Somalia

*I think of myself as black African. I feel welcome in Britain. This is my home now because it was my dream to live in the UK. I am good with languages and speak Somali, Swedish and English. I have been to parts of London and have met lots of different people, and have got to know some of them well. It's really nice and interesting to meet new people. I am a Muslim. My religion means everything to me because I am very happy with it. I respect that Britain is a Christian country because my religion says you have to respect any religion and its believers. I have never been inside a church. I only go to the mosque. The only places of worship that I know about are mosques and churches. I have a white English friend – his name is Michael. Yes, we are all equal, because we are all human beings. Besides, we are all going to die one day.*

## Cam from Vietnam

*I'm from Vietnam and think it is important for young asylum seekers and refugees to integrate well in Britain, because we can learn new things from everybody around us. Religion is quite important to me because I have a belief in Buddhism. This gives me peacefulness and the motivation to do anything. I think it is important for somebody like me to respect other people's religion because, if they respect mine, I should respect theirs. I go to a Buddhist temple every Sunday, but I have also visited churches from time to time. One of my friends is gay and I feel normal about that because everybody should be themselves. I don't have a problem with people who are different to me. We shouldn't judge anybody by their gender or skin colour or if they have a disability. Everybody is equal, because everyone is sharing the same earth and we all should help each other.*

## Aziz from Eritrea

*Actually, I identify myself as an Eritrean young boy. I feel welcome in this country and I'm happy to live here and build my future. According to me, it is very important to integrate in the community with other people different from myself. It is good to learn the different cultures and behaviour of other people. Religion is quite important to me. I'm an orthodox Tewahdo and I believe and practise my religion. I go to church in London as often as I can, but I am not always able to afford to pay the train ticket. My social worker has told me that they will help me with this.*

*I like going to church because I meet so many people from the country and from all age groups. In my opinion, there is little difference between culture and religion because culture is influenced by religion. I understand that Britain is a Christian country and I respect this because I too come from a diversified country in terms of religion. I have been to other Christian churches, different from my own, but I have never been to a mosque or a temple because I've never had the chance to visit one. I have many friends from different backgrounds. I find it easy to make friends because I speak four languages. Yes, I do think we humans are equal, because we are all mortal. Each person is going to taste death.*

## Cartan from Somalia

*I'm lucky because I speak different languages so this puts me in contact with many other types of people. I like talking to others. It helps that my English is good, which means that English people are able to speak to me. I'm Muslim, which is very important because Islam is everything you can ever ask for in the world. I practise Ramadan every year. I like discussing religion and listening to other people's views about God. I went into a Christian church once and thought it looked beautiful. This is something I would never have done in my own country. I believe all people are equal, but I don't like gay people. I don't like seeing them holding hands or kissing in public. That sort of behaviour is not allowed in my country.*

# Help – receiving help, offering help and helping yourself

This exercise was designed to help the young people think about the various types of help in ways they might not otherwise have considered by themselves outside discussion on the subject. We looked at help from three key perspectives.

» How to ask for help

» How to help others

» How to help yourself.

As part of the exercise, I provided the young people with a copy of Yonas's story – as featured in the first chapter of this book. To recap, Yonas was a 16-year-old boy from Eritrea who was worried about the well-being and safety of his mother because she had cried every day since he left. In many ways, Yonas's progression in life was curtailed because of the guilt he felt about his mother. As a result of his anguish, I asked the young people to consider the following question: '*If Yonas was your friend, what sort of help and support do you think you could give him?*'

## Biniam from Eritrea

*I would share with him my experiences and just tell him that things are going to change.*

## Rada from Vietnam

*If Yonas was my friend, I would take him to a Children's Support Centre or the nearest council, because I think they will find the best way to solve his problems.*

## Demsas from Eritrea

*Actually, my story is similar to his so in this kind of situation what you need is somebody to speak to, because when you speak about your worries you feel better – not only that you can get some solutions too. Talking to someone who can help you is a good thing.*

## Jamal from Sudan

*I would ask him to hang out with me and to play some games to make him forget what happened to him back home.*

111

## Guhaad from Somalia

*If Yonas was my friend, this would be my advice. If you are in the UK, you don't have to worry about anything as long as you are doing well. If you have made it safe to the UK, this means you are alive. Stay safe.*

The next question I asked the young people was: *'How best can your social worker/ 18plus personal adviser support you in your life?'*

## Hau from Vietnam

*My social worker helped me find a nice and safe place to live. Also, my key worker helped me to open a bank account and how to organise a shopping list. They are always there whenever I need support.*

## Demsas from Eritrea

*Not bad but they are not as supportive as under-18 social workers. When you are under 18, they care about you, but when you become 18 they say you are an adult and therefore you have to do everything by yourself.*

## Faheem from Sudan

*He's so good and always reminds me of my father.*

## Hanad from Somalia

*I'm under 18plus. My worker supports me very well and I'm happy with that.*

I then asked the young people: *'Could you be doing more to help yourself to build a good life in the UK?'*

## Aziz from Eritrea

*I will finish my education and I plan to go to a higher-level education. I just want to get a good job.*

## Rada from Vietnam

*I think I will learn more about everything in the UK to help build a good life through the lessons I have learnt at college and outside of college as well. I will attend the class on time and talk with everyone more, so that I can improve my English. I can learn more about everything around me through the people I meet.*

## Biniam from Eritrea

*Of course, at the moment I'm working hard to improve my English. My attendance is good. My ambition is to go to university and study something interesting.*

## Dung from Vietnam

*Yes, absolutely. I need to study harder if I am going to make a good career for myself.*

## Jamal from Sudan

*I will be doing anything and everything that I can to build my life in the UK. I will continue going to college to prove that I'm doing well. When I get 'Leave to Remain', I'll get a job and I'll save more money. I want to pass all my exams, because I want to go to university. I would like to stay safe 24/7, because London's streets are dangerous and there are many gangs.*

# What is your relationship like with money?

From my own direct work with young people, I know how important money is for them. Some are good with budgeting, while others are the complete opposite. Here I asked the young people to think about their finances and to ponder whether they were savers or spenders, while taking into account that they all lived off limited incomes.

## Dung from Vietnam

*I have been working for a few months already. The money I earn is enough for my life now. I usually save half my money and I put it in the bank. I spend the rest for living: food, travelling to work, internet and sometimes I go shopping with my friend. I don't have to pay any bill like electric, gas and council tax now, so I am quite good at saving money. However, I always have Vietnamese food for my meals and it's very expensive. I have been working hard to earn more money, because I would like to have a good life in the future. I would like to buy a new house and new car when I have my own family.*

## Biniam from Eritrea

*I've a good relationship with money because I don't smoke and drink. I just spend my money on important things. Sometimes I like to buy nice stuff like clothes, trainers and cooking materials. I have plans. I would like to go somewhere on a summer holiday. But I need to get a good job first, then I will save some money. One day I will buy a nice house and a car – things that will be important to me and my family. My advice to other young people about money is not to spend it smoking and drinking or buying unusual things.*

## Aziz from Eritrea

*I have a good relationship with money. When I have money, I can pay for whatever I need. If you work hard you can get all the money you need, but then it depends on how you end up spending it. In the future, when I have money, I want to put it to good use like putting it into housing or buying a car or joining a gym.*

*In this country, you can spend very quickly because there are so many bills to pay. If you have a car, you need to pay tax and insurance, so it's hard to save, but that is what I intend to do in the future.*

## Guhaad from Somalia

*I'm very good with money. I save £10 every week. I have saved for many things that I wanted. The first thing I saved for was my iPhone and after that I saved for a laptop, which cost £300, and then, another £250, for PS4.*

## Mohamed from Sudan

*I'm not good at saving money. I hardly get any money and, whenever I get it, I just spend it on food and things for my flat. It's important to save money because you won't know what's going to happen to you in the future. Money is fine, but if you play with it, you will burn yourself. So, if you play with it, you will get broke – so try to save some of it for your future.*

## Demsas from Eritrea

*I'm not bad with money. I can manage with the budget that I am given. Ideally, I would love to have enough money to buy a house that I could properly settle into. When I get my first job, my first goal is to get a mortgage so that I am paying into this rather than renting somewhere. I have a savings account that I can dip into if I have any problems. I advise all my friends to have a little pot of money that they can dip into in a crisis.*

## Rada from Vietnam

*I can't work now, so I still get money from my social worker. I use my money for buying food, clothes, personal items or going out with my friends. In the future, when I can earn money, I will spend more. I will buy a house, a car, have more clothes and travel the world. When I have a family, I will need to earn more money to take care of my family.*

# My beautiful country

Young people carry great affection towards their country of origin, often intermingled with resentment at having had to leave or fear of what they left behind. Then there are family members who they constantly think about. This exercise asked them to reflect on the beauty of their countries of origin, but also to think about the desired changes that need to take place in their homelands.

## Hau from Vietnam

*Ha Long Bay is one of the most beautiful places in Vietnam. It has a unique charm that cannot be seen anywhere else in the world. Vietnam also has many beautiful mountains including the Fansipan Peak, which everybody calls 'the roof of Indochina'. But, sadly, I had to leave Vietnam because of its unstable politics – there is no fairness in the country. Although I love my country, my life wasn't safe there. I don't agree with what the Vietnamese government is doing. The country has lost so many of its people to immigration. I still dream of visiting one day, but only if my life would be better there than before I left – I no longer want to live there.*

## Faheem from Sudan

*Sudan is one of the biggest countries in central Africa, bordered by Egypt to the north and with the Red Sea to northern Eritrea and Ethiopia. Sudan is famous for one of the longest and most beautiful rivers in the word – the River Nile. In addition to this, there are pyramids between Sudan and Egypt. Life is Sudan is tough, with a dog-eat-dog type of mind – so, if you are strong, you can live, but if you are not strong, then you won't survive. The government kills innocent people after they take their animals and property.*

*I left Sudan because of the Janjaweed (a militia that operates in western Sudan and eastern Chad) killed my mum and my uncle in front of me, so I ran away to find a safe place to live. The government doesn't care if all of the people in Sudan were to leave right now. I don't mind as long as I remain safe, but I still love my country and would like to return one day, provided it is safe. I would even like to die in my country.*

## Dung from Vietnam

*Vietnam has so many beautiful places. It has the landmark which is one of the highest buildings in the world. But despite the beauty of the place, I had to leave because my religion wasn't allowed in the country (Hoa Hao sect of Buddhism). Yes, it is true to say that the government will lose many workers and some talented people. Some factories will have to close because they won't have enough workers. I would like to return one day in the future, because my family all still live there. After all, this was the place where I was born.*

## Cartan from Somalia

*I'm from Somalia, which is located in east Africa. The capital city is called Mogadishu. We have a population of around 15 million. The whole country is Sunni Muslim. We used to have beautiful buildings – modern and ancient – but everywhere is all destroyed by civil wars. There are no longer many interesting places to visit, except maybe for the capital which has a beautiful peace park called Beerta Xor iyada – it's beautiful. We have two coasts – the northern coast with the Gulf of Aden and the north-eastern coast with the Indian Ocean. And two big rivers called Jubba and Shabeele. We have many beautiful beaches in Somalia. We have some wildlife animals, although most of these became extinct after the civil war. The majority of animals that you will see all the time are camels and goats.*

*Somalian people don't have a strong government. They don't have enough health services. Most of them don't have freedom. Most of the cities are dangerous, where you could get killed by walking around. The country does not have enough education and they also don't have enough clean drinking water.*

*Why did I leave? My reasons are different because the culture is different and difficult because you have to do things by force. At school, teachers beat you for the simplest of things. But my biggest problem is that the Al-Shabaab (a jihadist fundamentalist group) wanted me to work for them and I knew how dangerous this would be. I wouldn't go back to Somalia and live there again – but I would like to visit anytime I want – because I know I would never get there what I get in England. I would like to live in England forever.*

117

## Aziz from Eritrea

*My beloved country of Eritrea is located in the horn of Africa. It has the most beautiful of weather. The climate is good, almost all of the time. We have a nice culture, and what I mean by that is we are welcoming towards strangers. We don't create awkwardness. Instead, we like to make people feel at home. The reason why Eritreans leave their homeland is because of the regime of its government. Let me clarify that. In Eritrea, everyone has to join the military and it's boundless. It doesn't have an end. You have to serve your whole life. That makes it modern slavery in the name of national service.*

*The reason why I left Eritrea is because they accused me of a crime I hadn't done and put me in prison. They accused me of being a smuggler who was trying to get people across the border into Sudan. I was only 14. They had no evidence, but I still spent one week in the prison where they tried to beat a confession out of me. The cell was very crowded, with men of all ages. We all had to sleep on our sides for the entire night because there was little space. It was hot and dirty with lots of insects and mosquitoes. We were only given one meal a day of Ades (a lentil stew dish), but they made it so watery and without any taste. One day they were transporting us from one place to another. There weren't enough guards on duty. As we were going, some of the adult males attacked the guards and, when the fight broke out, I managed to run off.*

*Actually, the loss of youth to any country is a terrible loss, and Eritrea has suffered much because so many young people have left. A country without young people is a country that doesn't have a future. Yes, one day I would like to go back to Eritrea to see my parents, if I knew I would be safe.*

## Cam from Vietnam

*There are so many good things about my country, so I am going to tell some things about my country that I think might entice you to visit after you have read this. First of all, the food is plentiful and we cook so many different dishes from all over the world, but we also have our own special food that is unique to Vietnam – such as Banh mi (breakfast roll consisting of duck pate, spicy pickles and a fried egg), Pho (beef noodle soup) and Banh cuon (steamed rice rolls). Secondly, the landscape and the valleys are incredible in Vietnam.*

*People are generally happy and friendly with visitors, especially if you are a for-eigner and you need help. They will help you. However, the reason that people leave Vietnam is because of big political problems, as well as religious discrim-ination. People are leaving because they have no choice. As a result, my country has lost a lot of talented people because of these problems. I would love to one day return to my country if they have changed the rules, and if we had a demo-cratic government. That way there would be fewer problems for the people to face daily.*

# President for one day

This final exercise asked the young people to compile a list of things they would implement if they were the president of their country for a day – followed by a group exercise where they all contributed to drafting a list of things they would like to see changed in the UK if they were prime minister. So, first I asked: *'If you were president of your country for one day – what changes would you make to protect your country and its people from harm?'*

## Faheem from Sudan

1. *Free education to anybody under the age of 21.*

2. *For nobody to have guns – even the police.*

3. *Build more schools and hospitals.*

4. *Improve electricity and water supplies.*

## Biniam from Eritrea

1. *I would change the government because I want freedom in my country.*

2. *In my country we need more education.*

3. *In my country we need more elections.*

4. *I am afraid of going back to my country because of the police.*

## Rada from Vietnam

1. *For everybody to have equality – for somebody not to be able to use money to buy power.*

2. *Everybody has the right to freedom of speech.*

3. *Police must not use more than their power to force people.*

4. *For the government to give people more rights.*

5. *Better healthcare for people.*

## Demsas from Eritrea

1. *A better education system.*

2. *I would like to see changes in democracy.*

3. *I would do more about elections because there is no election.*

4. *I would change all the rules in Eritrea.*

5. *I would like to see better transportation in Eritrea.*

## Jamal from Sudan

1. *I would change the education system.*

2. *I would free all prisoners.*

3. *I would change the political system. What I mean by this is I would allow the people to choose who they would like to lead.*

4. *I would allow free press and democracy.*

5. *I would end corruption.*

6. *I would introduce constitution.*

Next, I asked the young people what they would do if they were the British prime minister for a day. The following list is their group answers.

1. *Legalise cannabis.*

2. *Offer quality educational opportunities – ESOL is not enough.*

3. *Make train fares cheaper.*

4. *Make changes in the prices of goods – make things cheaper.*

5. *Make changes in the Home Office in how they deal with the cases of refugees. They take a long time to make a decision, which is frustrating.*

6. *Build more houses – more schools and colleges.*

7. *Allow people who are over 18 and waiting for their refugee status to work and pay tax.*

8. *Give young people their refugee status quickly so that they can settle down and be helpful to the UK.*

9. *For there to be more jobs for young people.*

# Conclusion

My time with these young people showed me how they brimmed over with vitality and ideas, and had many hopes and ambitions for their futures. The group wasn't consumed with worry about Home Office delays or other bureaucracy. These are young people, who hadn't grown up in the UK, had made up time in their learning and showed an impressive knowledge of so many subjects, including history, geography, politics and modern culture. Here were young people who could express their opinions, share ideas, and get their point of view across about the dangers of drug misuse among young people and the follies and lethal dangers of knife and gang culture in London.

There was something refreshing about the students that made it easy to believe they had potential to make successes of their lives in the UK, based on their ability to reflect on and discuss a wide range of diverse topics. However, what was also apparent was their need to succeed in their ESOL course in order to progress onto a mainstream course that would lead to professional qualifications and employment. One of the young students from Sudan made me smile when he expressed how shocked he was to hear of someone who, having graduated from university, was unable to get a job compatible with their qualifications and was working instead in a coffee shop. The young man found this very hard to understand. However, the experience had not deterred him, because he was still hoping to study business at college.

# Introduction

This chapter looks at two polar-opposite countries, which will help contrast their services to those available in Britain. The first country is Ireland, which is a European country and Britain's closest neighbour and which offers a relatively different system to that of its neighbouring countries in Europe. The second country is Turkey, which is outside the EU and currently has the largest number of refugees in the world. A common theme between Ireland and Turkey is that both countries host Syrian refugees.

Terminology differs between the UK and Ireland in how young people are labelled, and this is explored in detail in this chapter along with opportunities, education, accommodation and future prospects. Results have often shown that Ireland is a welcoming place for refugees, but nevertheless a chronic shortage of accommodation and employment opportunities means that many may struggle. Turkey opened its borders and allowed in nearly five million refugees – a large percentage of which came from Syria. Life is difficult for Syrians in Turkey and this is coupled with much uncertainty. With the ongoing war in Syria, it is unclear whether they will be allowed to stay when the war ends. This chapter begins by looking at the largest comparative study ever carried out about refugees and asylum seekers.

# Comparative study

One of the largest comparative studies into young refugees was carried out by the European Migration Network and was published in 2018. The publication – *Approaches to Unaccompanied Minors Following Status Determination in the EU plus Norway* – looked at how European countries compared to each other. Its main aim was to look at countries who upheld the best interests of the child when allocating and providing services. This detailed analysis indicated that countries with smaller numbers of refugees and asylum seekers – eg Luxembourg and Slovenia – offered better services. Having said that, Germany, which has the highest number of refugees in Europe, is mainly at the forefront of providing good care and services. On the other hand, countries with smaller numbers – like Hungary and Poland – have, in the main, created hostile environments. However, it was clear in the findings of the report that almost every country struggled to provide exceptionally good provisions in terms of accommodation, finances and access to healthcare, including therapies for mental health issues.

The report highlighted a lack of specific requirements and policy for social workers and other practitioners – for example, knowledge of immigration and unaccompanied minors. This was identified as a challenge by several countries and it was acknowledged that it could potentially lead to gaps in the protection of unaccompanied minors. Britain, however, was noted as being one of the best countries with its safeguarding measures towards children and young people. Additionally, the study found that the UK and Finland were the only countries that have issued specific guidelines for those in charge of the care of unaccompanied minors and child victims of trafficking.

The study pointed out that the UK, Ireland and Italy were among the best countries who prepared young people for the transition to adulthood, with planning taking place up to one year before the young person's eighteenth birthday. Finland and the Netherlands were the best countries at being advocates of family reunification. In terms of providing good educational provision to young people, Germany was considered the best with choice and options, while Bulgaria only provided a limited education to those who were successful in their asylum applications. Many of the countries considered integration to be important, but Finland excelled at this. Bulgaria and Poland were singled out as not considering integration a priority. When it came to preparing packages of care for young people at risk of deportation or relocation back to their countries of origin, the Netherlands, Sweden, Belgium and France were much better at preparing young people than other countries.

# Ireland

Ireland can be a welcoming place for asylum seekers and refugees. Young people appear to integrate well with Irish citizens. The reason for this is the size of the country – London alone has nearly the same population as Southern Ireland. A further reason is the genuine warmth and friendliness of the Irish people, which can be contagious. It is lovely to think that young children arriving in Ireland will attend primary and secondary school, where they will develop Irish accents and play in national sports, including Gaelic football and hurling. They may even fall in love with an Irish person and get married one day. There is a downside, though, to living in Ireland. A national housing crisis means that only a select number will be socially housed – high rents bar many from ever entering the private sector (which is also stretched). The high cost of living, coupled with fewer jobs for unskilled workers, will eventually prove life-testing for many.

In October, 2019, 10 teenagers – including two 15-year-old boys – were among the 39 Vietnamese nationals found dead in a trailer in an industrial park in Grays, Essex, shortly after the lorry had arrived in the UK from Belgium on a ferry from Zeebrugge. Shock and horror at the gravity of this huge human loss was expressed in the media, alongside stories of how families had sold their farms or borrowed large amounts of money to pay the smugglers to take their loved ones away in the hope of a better life in Europe. If things had gone to plan, some of these people would have claimed asylum in the UK or Ireland, given that the smugglers charged with their deaths were from Northern Ireland.

There have been over 20,000 asylum seekers presumed drowned in the Mediterranean since 2014. Europe's image as a human rights champion has been put to the test. And Europe's limited humanitarian response to this crisis has made the Mediterranean Sea one of the deadliest in the world. However, when it comes to fully embracing refugees, the EU is the most polarised it has ever been. This is driven largely by the far-right and nationalist parties that are securing an increasing number of parliamentary seats. These once marginalised and extreme voices have been strengthened by three growing fears: cultural liberalisation, mass immigration and the perceived abandonment of national sovereignty, which has resulted in thousands of innocent people being left to die.

In Ireland, people generally encounter a sympathetic media stance towards asylum seekers and refugees, but the public discourse does not differ greatly to the UK. Ordinary members of the public do not understand the human complexities involved and many are switched off – preventing broader discussion. Traces of racism, ignorance and fear of difference have aroused criticism in some people – particularly the older generation, who speak out about how the Irish who left their country to seek a better life didn't get a free place to stay. They feel that asylum seekers and refugees should not be let in unless they are willing to work and find their own accommodation, like the Irish did when they emigrated during times of economic hardship and civil war.

Between 3000 and 4000 asylum-seeking families have arrived in Ireland in recent years from African countries, the Middle East and Albania. Approximately 6000 people live in these 35 centres across Ireland – 2000 of whom are children and young people. Most asylum seekers and refugees entering Ireland are accommodated in the Republic (Southern Ireland). A smaller number reside in Northern Ireland, which has a dedicated residential unit for unaccompanied, separated, trafficked and asylum-seeking children and young people who have arrived from various parts of the world, including: Somalia, Sudan, Iran, Afghanistan, Zimbabwe and Syria.

Children trafficking is as much a problem in Ireland as it is in the UK. Each year, more and more Vietnamese children are trafficked. Some of these are in Ireland – hidden and undocumented. Some are placed in cannabis-growing houses and used as cheap labour, where they are paid a few euros a day. Campaigners are aware of these crimes and Irish aid workers currently go to Vietnam to deliver English programmes to help as many Vietnamese children learn to speak English as possible. It is felt that this will have a major impact on the number of children and young people who are trafficked in the future, because this will empower them to break free from slavery and injustice.

In Ireland, the term 'Separated Children' is preferred to UASC, because it removes the 'asylum-seeking' emphasis and reinforces the notion that these are children who have been separated from their families, carers or guardians. They became separated either at the beginning of their journey or during it, mainly in Greece and Turkey. It is recognised that when they arrive in a new country, they must instantly address the sudden loss of attachment that parents and primary caregivers provide. Being suddenly cut off from this type of emotional warmth results in their mental health suffering.

## Torture

During their journey to Europe, many migrants become victims of torture, enslave-ment and sexual violence. Victims of torture often come from Zimbabwe, the Democratic Republic of the Congo, Afghanistan, Nigeria, Pakistan, Iran, Iraq and Syria. Many of these minors are trafficked and bear physical scarring and psychological disturbances. The UN's definition of torture is:

*any act by which severe pain or suffering, whether physical or mental, is intentionally inflicted on a person for such purposes as obtaining from him or a third person information or a confession, punishing him for an act he or a third person has committed or is suspected of having committed, or intimidating or coercing him or a third person, or for any reason based on discrimination of any kind, when such pain or suffering is inflicted by or at the instigation of or with the consent or acquiescence of a public official or other person acting in an official capacity. It does not include pain or suffering arising only from, inherent in or incidental to lawful sanctions.*

(APT and CEJIL, 2008, pp 10–11)

Forms of torture include whipping the soles of feet, water torture, starvation, kidnap-ping and being forced to witness family members being raped or murdered. Sometimes the act of getting a person, including children, to strip naked automatically makes them feel vulnerable and powerless. Sexual violence often occurs among women coming from African countries. Other victims have endured electric shocks to the soles of their feet – something that is not always picked up in health examinations. Organ harvesting among young men from Afghanistan is also a frequent occurrence – it is not uncommon for young men, from the age of 17 upwards, to have sold a kidney and be cheated over the money they were promised and how they were left with no aftercare.

Torture causes shame and taboo and is never easy to talk about. Survivors are also affected by what is known as the 'triple trauma affect', in the sense that they have left their homelands and have had to settle in a new country with a different language and cultural norms and values. Thankfully, there are organisations that help; including Spiraci in Dublin, who specialise in working with victims of torture. Referrals to the service come from GPs and solicitors who are aware that torture occurred. The service offers counselling and family therapy (a type of psychotherapy that can help family members improve communication and resolve conflicts). This has proved successful to those who endured trauma before or during their journey, including those who experienced sexual violence during some part of their life and/or female genital mutilation. Psycho-social education around the effects of trauma is discussed, including its physical manifestations. People are taught coping mechanics and how best to support family members struggling with traumatic flashbacks.

The service believes in working with people's strengths and encourages empowerment to men and women whose lives have literally being turned upside down – including those who feel they have lost everything. During family therapy, gender roles and cultural scripts are re-enacted and sometimes challenged – for example, the idea that men are expected to work while women are expected to stay at home. New cultural experiences can often put strain on relationships, which in turn affects the children – although sometimes the children speak better English than their parents and have to act as interpreters. The service also carries out medical and legal reports on separated children in order to assist in their asylum applications – as well as classes in English and independent living skills.

During my Irish research, I was told a story about a separated young person who had been tortured and was referred to the service. He would dissociate to the point where he would collapse at school and he felt deeply ashamed that it was happening. He engaged well in play therapy (a form of treatment that helps children and families to express their emotions, improve their communication and solve problems). The boy used metaphors to be able to show what happens when he collapses. The boy drew a picture of a cage, telling his therapist that he wanted to be inside the cage where he would be totally safe. Beside the cage, he drew his father. He then described his father as a lion to denote how he considered him a protective and strong man, who tried his best to protect him from the monster who harmed him.

The boy's therapist focused on the boy's strengths and looked at his courage and ability to survive such stressful and physical painful experiences. Trauma and its effects were explained to him in simple terms, enabling him to understand what happens to the body when trauma is involved – hence, he was able to understand his fainting episodes. The young person was given advice and support about how to self-regulate his emotions when becoming overwhelmed by thoughts of the past.

## Accommodation

Separated young people in Ireland are allocated foster placements. Sometimes, young people struggle to function and are re-traumatised by this system, particularly because of the lengthy waiting time for an outcome in the asylum process. If foster placements break down (and they often do), young people are moved to short-term residential placements (like children's homes) before being transferred again into direct provision accommodation when they reach 18 (more about direct provision in a moment). However, separated children appear to integrate much better than adults. Attending school, where friendships are easily formed, is a prime reason for this. Once the young person reaches 18, their social work support is cut off. There appears to be far less assistance in Ireland for separated children once they reach adulthood compared to the UK and its leaving care provision. The young people who are part of Children's Services and are then removed from the system upon their eighteenth birthday struggle with the fact that strong bonds of trust are broken with their foster carers and other professional relationships.

Regretfully, it is not uncommon to hear of young people aged 18 and over who are moved out of foster care and placed in hostels with drug abusers. This travesty is caused by the chronic shortage of suitable social housing in Ireland. The Irish government is currently under pressure to cater for the rising number of people claiming international protection in Ireland. They are even considering using defence forces' accommodation, as well as some of its training and warehouse facilities. In fact, the housing crisis in Ireland often means that new arrivals are now placed in emergency bed and breakfast hotels and hostels, because everywhere else is full.

There are two main forms of provision in Ireland where asylum-seeking and refugee families are accommodated.

### 1. Emergency Reception Orientation Centres (EROC)

Syrian refugee programmes started in Ireland when the Department of Justice sent officials to refugee camps in Greece and Turkey before agreeing to accept families. Most of the people in the camps knew nothing about Ireland. A few had heard about St Patrick and his association with Ireland. Nearly all of them referred to their mobile phones and used Google to learn more about the country that would become their new home. Many Syrians come from good backgrounds and are professional, well-educated people, but owing to years of civil war have endured hardship and heartache and many suffer from PTSD. Syrians value education and want to work and be an asset in the community.

Families and children (programmed refugees) are placed in EROCs where they can stay for up to six months or longer before being housed by the Red Cross in various towns across Ireland. All migrants in the programme cohort are given five years' LTR upon arrival. Many EROCs are former hotels that closed after the economic crash in 2009. Full board is given because most of the EROC establishments do not have cooking facilities. Welcoming committees are in place in areas where EROCs are located. Local volunteers form committees designed to help the new arrivals get to know their new neighbourhoods. Local church groups and schools have also played their part in helping in whatever they can to ensure that newcomers are made to feel welcome to Ireland. Social outings get organised by local community groups, including taking young people to football matches or playing pool.

Integration has been smooth for many of the refugees, who are Muslim, and it is not an uncommon sight to see them celebrating Christmas with residents in their neighbourhood – and vice versa when it comes to Islamic celebrations of Ramadan and Eid. Islam is the third largest religion in Ireland, so therefore there are mosques and prayer centres where the refugees go to pray. One of the volunteers at an EROC centre in the West of Ireland told me a beautiful story of how he once saw a Muslim woman and the local priest praying together in the local Catholic church. The church was seen by the woman as a holy place of worship and she would often visit by herself to pray and sit in silence. This peacefulness was deemed therapeutic for a woman who had seen and experienced so much human suffering, death and hardship.

Local communities have said they have got used to seeing refugees around local towns and that they would miss them when they are relocated elsewhere. Many friendships are formed, and it has not gone unnoticed that refugees are also a boost to the local economy with money spent in supermarkets and charity shops. Staff and volunteers help refugees open bank accounts and complete job applications, forms for housing and/or any legal paperwork. English lessons are offered, as well as support and guidance in preparing for life in Ireland when they move into their own accommodation. Most of the refugees, including those who are in their late teens and early adulthood, are eager to work and want to pay Ireland back for being good to them. Some find work in barber shops, garages and meat factories. Some young men over 18 have even signed up for the army reserves, after discovering that the Irish army is very different to the Syrian army.

## 2. Direct provision accommodation

Accommodation in direct provision establishments resembles EROCs in the sense that they mainly consist of disused hotels that have been converted especially to house families, children and single individuals. Direct provision centres are run by private contractors, including the multinational prison company, Aramark. A stark reality is that asylum seekers can live in direct provision accommodation for six or seven years before they receive a decision on their asylum claim.

Adults live off a government allowance of less than 40 euros a week and an allowance of less than 30 euros is allocated to each child. Full board is provided to all the residents, although a few places allow them to do their own cooking – this is usually triggered by residents' protestations. Other common complaints about direct provision accommodation include having no privacy, very little dignity, poor play areas for children, inadequate gym facilities, residents being made to feel useless and experiencing a poor attitude among staff towards them. There are also psychological effects including depression and suicide ideation as a result of living in cramped, poor accommodation – at least two people have died by suicide in recent years.

The picture is not entirely bleak, however. While there are some badly run direct provision centres, there are equally some run by staff who carry out their duties professionally and who passionately care about the rights and entitlements of asylum seekers and refugees. Many staff work closely with parents and their children and offer multiple services including mental health support, helping with housing applications, social welfare entitlements, education and employment and ensuring they are registered with a GP.

Several external services are carried out with clients, including constructive activities, cultural nights and access to short courses – enabling integration in the community. When speaking to staff in Dublin who work with young asylum seekers in direct provision, they told me that most young people want to go to school and learn because they value education and securing a good job. Colleges have allowed certain criteria for young asylum seekers and refugees to enrol, including allowing access to mainstream courses providing the applicant's English literacy skills are good. Level 3 qualifications can lead to college and university places. People can succeed provided they work hard and are determined. However, it is often found that young asylum seekers and refugees are not given enough information about Level 3 courses in IT, healthcare and nursing.

Criticisms exist about how some families remain in direct provision for many years while seeking housing, despite having been granted asylum. Many landlords react badly upon hearing of a family who receive housing assistance payments (the equivalent of housing benefit in the UK) and prefer tenants who are able to personally pay the rent.

## LGBT community Black Pride parade

All asylum seekers and refugees face hostility and discrimination at some point in their lives. But those who are gay have to endure an extra layer of condemnation because of their sexual orientation. This can be as equally severe from members of their own community (families, even) as it is from strangers. Many refugees come from countries where homosexuality is illegal and where the rights of the LGBT community are not recognised in the slightest. Some come from countries where the death penalty is in place for practising gay people, including Afghanistan, Iran, Somalia and Sudan.

How liberating it must be for young adults – men and women – to find themselves in a position where they can be open and feel safe living in a European country that has legal rights to protect them. It is even more liberating for them to join annual pride marches and be free to show everybody who they really are, without feeling the need to hide their sexuality for fear of repercussions from the law. Several young gay and lesbian asylum seekers and refugees are part of Black Pride Ireland (for people who do not identify as white), which was set up as an alternative to the largely white mainstream LGBT movement. In recent years, several have taken part in the annual Black Pride march that takes place each summer in Galway, including some black trans women.

## Discrimination and Islamophobia

Despite a mainly positive press in Ireland towards migrants – and irrespective of the reporting on the current accommodation crisis (in general) and how this affects asylum seekers and refugees – the occasional protest against their arrival and stay in Ireland is not completely prevented. Many of these protests have carried nasty messages requesting the Irish government to stop dumping asylum seekers in 'their back yards', as if these human beings were rubbish. In other places, far-right groups have tried to stir up hatred by talking about Muslims in derogatory terms and trying to spread untrue stories that state Muslims advocate beheadings of non-Muslims. A few local newspapers and radio stations jump on the bandwagon if they feel there is a news story to grab people's attention. After one EROC resident wrote to a local newspaper complaining about the poor quality of the food they were expected to eat, the response was: *'If they don't like it, why don't they go back to where they came from?'*

# Turkey

The situation in Syria is the worst humanitarian crisis since the Rwandan genocide in 1997. Since the civil war started in 2011, the country has seen the exodus of over

8 million people. Over half a million people are missing, 6 million are displaced within the country and over 13 million are in need of humanitarian assistance. Many Syrian refugees fled the country and went to neighbouring countries including Lebanon and Jordan, but the largest number found safety in Turkey, which is now home to 5 million refugees – the largest number worldwide – of which over 3.5 million are Syrian. This compares to Pakistan (the second largest) with 1.5 million and Germany (the third largest) with over 1 million refugees.

Turkey states that it has spent 45 million American dollars supporting the refugees, with the EU investing a further 2 billion euros in humanitarian funding. Additional funding has also been provided by the UN and international charities such as Save the Children. As a result of the large number of Syrians finding sanctuary in Turkey, the number seeking asylum in Europe has significantly fallen in recent years.

Life in Turkey is not easy, however. The UN estimates that 65 per cent of Syrian households in Turkish cities live close to or below the poverty line. Yet Syrians like Turkey and view it positively in terms of being able to integrate and practise their religion. The likelihood is that most will remain there, although 'returning home under safe conditions' continues to be a solution for some refugees. Deportation back to Syria at the present time could certainly mean death for many women, children and those from the LGBT community. Despite what Turkey has done for Syrians, the country still faces the prospect of US sanctions over its military operation against the Kurds in Syria.

# Inside Turkey

I interviewed a charity worker who worked with Syrian refugees and obtained an inside point of view on the support available to Syrians currently living in towns and cities across Turkey.

> *Initially upon arriving, Syrian refugees were placed in specially erected tents, but over 90 per cent are now living in settled accommodation in towns and cities across the country. Some include whole families. However, it is hard to find a home – poor accommodation in deprived areas. Rents are high. For example, some places may cost 1200 TL per month and for this you could be living in a basement flat – overcrowded with up to seven to ten people who share the rent money – but this does not include heating and electricity. In fact, there might not be heating in such places – little sunlight and poor bathroom and kitchen facilities.*

*There are no accommodation allowances given and no welfare state payments, although they have access to free healthcare. Syrians are expected to earn their living and are allowed to open bank accounts. Many are exploited and endure bad working conditions in low-paid and unskilled jobs in factories and catering. Syrians need a work permit, which employers are supposed to provide – many don't because they feel Syrians don't need insurance because healthcare is free for them in Turkey. Jobs consist of a minimum of 12-hour shifts – earning 2000 TL, with overtime often paid cash-in-hand to avoid taxes.*

*Some leave – an example given to me was of a young couple who went to Belgium but decided to return illegally to Turkey because of the religious aspect. They said that they much prefer working in a Muslim country than in Belgium. In Turkey, they were able to adapt better to Turkish traditions because of their religion. The woman could wear her hijab without any problem. They disapproved of sex education in schools for children in Belgium. There are others too who are torn in their values. On the one hand, they express satisfaction in the freedom they experience in Turkey by not feeling suppressed like they did in Syria. While on the other hand, they lament that Turkey is not like living in a Muslim country when acknowledging aspects of its secular society.*

*Many young Syrians dream of a life in Britain or some other part of Europe; however, it has become much more difficult to leave Turkey. The most widely used route of migration to Greece is via Izmir, a coastal town in Turkey, but the chances of getting caught by coastal staff on either side are very high. If caught at the coast, a brief period of detention ensues before being returned to Turkey. Successful entry via a smuggler costs between $200–300, and those who are lucky enough to make it through to the mainland end up in the asylum camps on one of the Greek Islands. One of these camps is on the Greek island of Lesbos, already home to several thousand migrants in the infamous Moria camp; known as the worst refugee camp on earth – rife with stabbings and reports of children as young as ten who attempt suicide. For those lucky enough to have the financial means to continue with their journey in the hope of reaching Europe, a further $2000 may buy your passage.*

*Status wise, Syrians are not considered as 'refugees' in Turkey and face an uncertain future. Currently they are allowed to stay indefinitely (as determined on their registration card given upon entry), but this can be revoked at any time. Gaining citizenship, even after five years, proves difficult for many. There are strict criteria focused upon education, skills and financial independence. Those who are successful, though, have to pay $2500 for their citizenship. It* *is estimated that up to 170,000 Syrians have been given citizenship in Turkey and that many of these come from teaching or engineering backgrounds, which has filled deficits in the job market.*

*Many Syrians are considered second-class citizens in Turkey, but the majority want to stay in Turkey. This wasn't the case at first, but slowly discrimination began to set in through social media as a result of the Turkish government announcing their money plans to help Syrians. Then they became 'visible' in communities who often disapproved of their dominant culture – for example, the way women dress in black hijabs. People were vocal in their prejudice towards them and often wrote 'we want them to go back to their own country. We don't want them to integrate here.' Others claim that peace in Turkey is jeopardised since the arrival of the Syrians. Some say, 'I won't let my children go out and play on the street with those Syrians.'*

*A lot of this prejudice comes from within communities that are often poor, with deprived housing and high unemployment statistics. It is felt by observers that Syrians are used as a scapegoat for blaming things on them that are simply not fair or true. It is a little like certain myths and misconceptions which exist in the UK for those who think that asylum seekers and refugees take away jobs from British people and have far better access to social housing and welfare benefits than that of some natives. Some Turkish people see visiting Arabs from Saudi Arabia, Lebanon and Qatar in cities like Istanbul and wrongly think they are Syrians. This has led to a myth that the Syrians have sufficient income to live very comfortably in Turkey, which is not the true reality of their lives. In fact, the opposite is often true.*

# Interviewing Abdullah

Abdullah (25) is the second eldest of a family of nine and has lived in Istanbul since 2018. Except for his older brother who lives in Turkey, his parents and seven other siblings are still in Syria. Abdullah suffered several injuries in the war. There are still fragments of the warplanes in his body and he will require further operations to remove these at some point. Abdullah said that everything is difficult for his health and that there is no help available in Turkey. He works in a confectionary factory, which he considers to be exploitation. He currently earns 1500 TL per month (approximately £200) and goes to work at seven in the morning and sometimes works until midnight if there is overtime, because otherwise the salary is not enough to pay rent, electricity, food and travel. He is far from his family because of the war and knows he can never go back there, but his family are fine. He says he would prefer to leave Turkey, but Syrians need a visa to travel. Ideally, Abdullah wants to go to Europe and live a better life.

Abdullah was aged 14 when the war started. Up until that point, everything was beautiful in Syria, *'but I was young and did not know the true meaning of life'*. He filmed the bombings on a daily basis and over a four-year period made programmes documenting Russia's war crimes, which have been shown on Syrian television and widely on YouTube. Abdullah photographed serious bombings and witnessed horrific injuries, including acid attacks. He considered himself a free media activist, who did not follow any network, but his work was distributed on all channels, free of charge and for humanitarian purposes. The goal was for all people to see what was happening in Syria with the crimes of Bashar al-Assad.

Abdullah made many dangerous videos during the bombings. No journalist was able to pick up on things like he did, but he constantly lived in danger because he saw death every minute. *'Fear always chased me.'* Abdullah, who is a Sunni Muslim, reflected, *'Assad is unjust and does not allow Muslims to live and operate as well as the Shiite and Alevi sects. Sheikhs are not allowed to talk about anything – any person talking about politics is arrested.'*

## Abdullah's story in his own words

*I will talk about things I saw with my own eyes. Security forces intervene in house searches for intense revenge. Women are raped in front of their husbands. I will talk about the bombing a little – the intensity of the bombing at night. We never knew who died. We couldn't go out at night-time. Instead, we went in the morning. We entered the houses that were bombed at night. We found scary things including the bodies of children. All this revenge because the poor people came out and demanded freedom. Houses were destroyed, mosques were destroyed, as well as heritage sites. Many children now live without mothers. Many women have lost their children. Many men have lost their wives. In Syria, the war is not only artillery bombing. Rather it is a war of starvation as revenge against the people. For me, I lost a lot of my friends and I have seen others get injured many times. My dreams of a happy future will never be fulfilled. Sometimes in Syria, we prefer to die because of this terrible, difficult life.*

*I was born in Syria in the city of Homs. I lived many beautiful days in this city during my childhood. Demonstrations against injustice began all over the city of Homs, before it extended to all other Syrian cities. I was 14 years old, very young.*

*I knew nothing but I began to demonstrate with all the people. I began to chant for freedom, but I was young and innocent. The number of martyrs began to increase daily. I began to hate this unjust rule. I began to know the meaning of freedom. I decided to go out in all demonstrations against injustice. The unjust began to respond to the demonstrators with live bullets. They stormed the city with military tanks in the attempt to stop these peaceful demonstrations. I lost three young friends, who died as a result of shelling on their homes.*

*More military tanks entered the city, bombing houses, mosques and ancient archaeological sites. Day by day, the humanitarian situation got worse. The regime did not find a solution to stop these protests. Assad decided to besiege the city. He forbade everything – food, medicine and essential materials. The war had truly started. People began to feel hungry. There was no gas, no medicine, and no nutrition for children. Let me ask you a question. How would you feel if you were sitting in a cafe and a tank shell comes and explodes right in front of you? How difficult and frightening would that be? Every day, I lived in this moment. Many friends died beside me. I saw children die in front of my eyes and I could not protect them from this unjust aggression.*

*The bombing is daily and does not stop. The Russian warplanes intervened. They started killing us. I lived in terror every day. It felt like I was waiting for my death as a result of the intense bombing from the planes, which contained all kinds of internationally prohibited weapons. I decided to do anything to document these crimes committed by the Syrian regime with Russian support. My family were more afraid for my safety, though none of them prevented me from doing anything.*

*I started working in the media field. I was very enthusiastic because I wanted to report the injustices. I woke up early every day to document the shelling and the number of martyrs who fell every hour. I did not have a camera, so I used my mobile phone to upload photos and videos to social media. I had a lot of followers on Facebook. I continued doing this until I got injured for the first time during a bombing. I stayed in bed for four months. I didn't move until I recovered.*

*Although I recovered, my health was much worse than before. So too was the condition of many of the people of the city, because of the lack of health and food items. Our bodies became very tired due to a lack of nutrition. Dozens of martyrs died because of the bombings and some died because of starvation. There were no hospitals in the city big enough to cope with this large number of people. Not all of the medical supplies were available. I know many young children died due to a lack of food and medical supplies.*

*More time passed. Every minute of every day, the fear of death haunted me until I suffered a second injury. This time I stayed in bed for three months. I started to feel that death was chasing me. Thankfully, I recovered and my determination remained for my work. I continued to take pictures and videos of the war. Did you know that no Arab country has intervened to help the people from this war?*

*Some friends decided to help me buy a camera, which enabled me to do many things in my work. A whole year passed. Nothing changed. The tragedy continued to get worse. One day, I went to buy bread at seven in the morning. I was surprised when an artillery shell landed next to me. I fell to the ground and lost consciousness. I was hospitalised and woke up at 11.30 that night surrounded by my friends and family. I did not feel much pain due to general anaesthesia, and everybody was telling me not to worry. And then the effect of the anaesthesia began to wear off. I began to feel a lot of pain everywhere in my body. I was screaming in pain, asking for death until the pain stopped in my body. I stayed in bed and could not walk for five months. I will never be able to forget those painful moments and this sadness. I lost so many of my friends. I also lost many of my relatives in the war. I saw things that cannot be described.*

*One day, the regime began threatening to demolish the city over the heads of its residents or to get out of it. We had no second option. The people who refused to stay in the city began to negotiate with any party affiliated with the United Nations in order to protect those who wanted to leave to the north of the city of Idlib. Dozens of buses came to the city in order to displace every person who refused to remain under the unjust rule. I decided to leave and go to Idlib. It was not a good life in Idlib, because of the intensity of the Russian aerial bombardment there, so I decided to go to Turkish lands where I could have more surgery to treat my injuries. There was no safe way to enter Turkey. I started trying to enter for three months. I was arrested several times by the border guards. I was beaten and insulted because I had entered the Turkish lands in an illegal way. But I survived this too.*

*Despite me telling you this story, I can swear to you that it is only 20 per cent of the moments that I lived in Syria. I will never forget those sad, scary nights that passed without electricity, no lighting, and hearing the Russian planes coming to deliver their loads over our heads. The screams of the women and children linger in my mind. Eight years I lived in the war. I cannot forget those horrible moments. I cannot forget my friends who died before my eyes.*

# Abdullah's brother

Abdullah said that when the system takes revenge on its people, it claims things that burn the heart. They kill young children before the eyes of their mothers. Being tortured to death is a crime that has never before occurred in the Syrian people's history. They put men in prison and torture them to death – some die within days, some after a whole year and some die after five years. Very few people come out alive. The closest example that Abdullah spoke about was his brother, Mohammed, who was arrested in 2011 and spent three years under torture.

Mohammed (29), though, is one of the lucky ones, because he, too, is a survivor of the Assad government. But he tasted death in all sorts of ways in Sednaya Prison, known as the 'prison of death'. The prison was a human slaughterhouse. The rooms were small, made of iron, and housed 32 young men. Prisoners never saw the sun. During the torture episodes, the prisoner had to kneel with their face to the wall and was never allowed to see his jailer. Torture consisted of slapping and kicking. Sometimes the person was placed inside the tyre of a car, rendering them powerless and unable to move. Then they were beaten with sticks and cable belts, resulting in the shredding and cracking of skin until bones were exposed. Electric shocks were also used, as well as the deprivation of sleep, food and drink for long periods. The burning of cigarettes on the skin and solvents was also used.

As a teenager, Mohammed entered compulsory military service. He was serving in the Assad regime's army before the outbreak of the Syrian revolution. When he saw how the Assad regime suppressed and killed civilians, he and some of his friends tried to escape but were arrested. Mohammed said:

*Time has no meaning when you stand withered and helpless, powerless and trembling – watching someone you love have their body beaten to a pulp, and words cannot describe the moment you realise not a breath will leave his lips ever again.*

After his release from Sednaya, Mohammed weighed a mere 34kg and was sick with tuberculosis, scabies and diarrhoea for years. During his time in prison, he said he always felt the presence of God, before adding, '*The criminal who tortures is under the control of Assad. He is made to carry out his orders – he has to forget about religion, himself and the existence of God.*'

Mohammed finds life difficult in Turkey, but considers it far better than living under Assad – a life of bombing and destruction and seeing blood every day. Anybody who dares to go back to Syria will get arrested, detained and possibly murdered.

Mohammed questioned out loud, *'Can you imagine what they would do to me?'* Every day he publishes Assad crimes on Facebook and other social media. *'Bashar al-Assad is a war criminal who kills civilians. Innocent and poor people are arrested because they went against him and because of his fascist dictatorship government. Demonstrators were tracked down, bombed, destroyed and killed.'*

The future is unknown. There are still hundreds of thousands of refugees in camps and thousands of detainees in prisons. And the genocide continues daily. Mohammed thinks that many racists and countries stand by Assad – who uses the pretext of suppressing terrorism as a means of clinging to power, including Iran and Russia – and his criminal gang. *'Assad serves the interests of Russia and Iran in selling oil and gas by occupying the country.'* Mohammed received treatment and counselling in Istanbul for PTSD and depression. His mental health is now stable and he is currently rebuilding his life.

# Conclusion

In this chapter, readers will have discovered the different lifestyles that Syrian refugees have in Ireland and in Turkey. Here are people who shared many similar experiences in their homeland, but now, in many cases, live polar-opposite lifestyles. Those in Ireland on resettlement programmes may be in education or employment. An emphasis on learning English and integration has taken its toll on their emotional stability and well-being. They are able to make plans for the future while recovering and healing from the ordeals of war, although life in direct provision accommodation is often far from being satisfactory.

Life for Syrian refugees in Turkey remains uncertain with regard to their length of stay, and many face harsher living conditions than those in Ireland. Admittedly, Syrian Muslims appreciate the advantage of living in a Muslim country, although they are treated unfairly by the system and are often discriminated against by the Turkish people. Further uncertainty looms because of Turkey's sudden decision to open the borders with Greece, and Bulgaria reneging on the financial promises it made with the EU to contain the flow of asylum seekers coming to Europe – although this may appear to be the answer for thousands of refugees who long to leave Turkey and live in Europe. However, those brave enough to attempt hazardous sea crossings have been threatened with armed soldiers, tear gas and smoke grenades. Those who successfully make the journey into Europe, however, are guaranteed a life of living within a hostile environment, rendering their existence to perpetual poverty and deprivation that will test their mental endurance to the limit.

# Chapter 8 | Young adults

## Introduction

This chapter looks at the lives of young adult refugees and asylum seekers in Britain, paying particular attention to those who are not care leavers and therefore living without access to the services and entitlements afforded to those who arrived in the UK before their eighteenth birthday. In the previous chapter, you will have read Abdullah's story of his current life in Turkey as he battles the trauma of enduring war in Syria for many years. Here is a young man who dreams of coming to Britain, where he believes he will be able to live a good life and may even be afforded the opportunity of getting a job in the media as a photographer. Such dreams can only become a reality through hard work and determination and, even then, only occur in a small number of cases. As you will see in this chapter, the odds are stacked against young adults like Abdullah from the start, because Britain does not make it easy for success and advancement. Indeed, many hardships are guaranteed as part of the asylum journey.

## Care leavers

Young people who have been Children in Need for at least 13 weeks prior to their eighteenth birthday are entitled to leaving care services. As I mentioned in an earlier chapter, triple planning takes place (between Children's Services and the 18plus team) six months prior to the young person's birthday. A plan is devised and put in place to assist the young person's smooth transition into adulthood. Some young people manage the change easily, while others struggle. This depends on the length of time they have been in the country, their level of English, resilience and whether or not they have lived independently prior to their eighteenth birthday.

Care leavers are entitled to support up until their twenty-fifth birthday. Young people remain accommodated by the local authority until their twenty-first birthday, although a few sign themselves out of care once they receive their refugee status. This is mainly because they have developed very good independent living skills and no longer wish to feel restricted by having to remain in contact with professional services. However, most avail themselves of leaving care services until at least their twenty-first birthday and receive a wide range of support from their 18plus advisers, including financial support for driving lessons and clothing allowances.

When they sign themselves out of the care system, some young people move to other parts of the UK to live with older brothers, uncles or friends. However, if a young person does this and later changes their mind, they are still eligible to request help from their 18plus team who will re-open their case and provide support and guidance with key issues – mainly housing and mental health needs. Likewise, local authorities will continue to support young people who are over 18 and awaiting the result of their asylum application. Some local authorities will continue to support young people with failed applications up until the age of 21, although some teams withdraw support from young people who have reached ARE and have had a negative Human Rights Assessment (as previously mentioned in Chapter 5). While this may be viewed as punitive, the response from 18plus workers indicates they often find this emotionally draining. Therefore, they do everything in their power to encourage the young person to either lodge a fresh application for asylum and/or, although far from being ideal, take up the Section 4 Home Office support of accommodation and financial assistance when there are no other options.

A care leaver's grant of up to £2000 is available for young people who want to move from local authority accommodation to privately rented and advance towards greater independence. However, there is strict eligibility criteria. The young person must have received their refugee status or equivalent, have very good independent living skills, speak good English and be in stable employment. They also need to be able to prove that they could manage a tenancy, declare their income and produce wage slips before the local authority will act as a guarantor. The grant can be used towards buying furniture and other essential accessories.

Like triple planning before a young person's eighteenth birthday, there is what is called a 'Personal Housing Plan' that starts after a young person's twentieth birthday. This plan aims to guide them towards planning for their long-term futures. After the age of 21, young people move out of accommodation provided by the local authority. Many teams have a housing officer who will assist them to look at privately rented accommodation and social housing. The housing officer will liaise with landlords, council housing departments and social housing organisations, attend interviews and panel meetings, and generally streamline the whole process.

The majority of young refugees aged between 21 and 25 years old generally do well living independent lives; however, even the most resilient are still contacted by their personal adviser every six to eight weeks. This can be a telephone call, WhatsApp message, Skype call, email or, if needed, face-to-face contact, although the latter is reserved for those struggling with their housing or those experiencing mental health issues such as PTSD, depression and sometimes psychosis. Those within the 21–25 years age group are also protected in the same way as those in the 18–21 years bracket – in the sense that if they sign themselves out of care, they are entitled to return up until their twenty-fifth birthday.

Many of the young people I met often complained about their level of contact with their 18plus advisers – with several feeling that they hardly ever saw or heard from them. Admittedly, this has come from those who are early into their transition to adulthood and have previously been used to a more proactive service from their social workers. Based on the statutory requirements laid out by 18plus teams, the criticism does seem to be unfounded in the sense that support is in place to be given to all young people but the more direct face-to-face work takes place with those who particularly struggle with life in the UK, including those who are unemployed and/or have chronic mental health needs. In fairness to 18plus teams, they feel it is their duty to empower young people as much as they can and that means giving indirect guidance and support to young people that enables them to do things for themselves.

Upon closer inspection, it is estimated that 80 per cent of young adults with refugee status live fairly successful lives by integrating well in society, learning English, finding employment and generally contributing to society. Ten per cent do exceptionally well and, in this group, it is not unusual to hear of young people doing well at university or starting up their own businesses. The remaining 10 per cent are, unfortunately, those who commit crimes and end up in prison, usually for county lines offences (drug dealing) and sexual offences that are usually around the age of consent. It is noted that this is prevalent among some young people from Iran, Afghanistan and some African countries, where the age of consent is not specified because marriage is largely required in these countries before sex is allowed.

# New arrivals

After arriving in the country, an adult asylum seeker will be issued with an immigration bail letter. This requires him or her to periodically report directly to the Home Office to ensure his or her whereabouts are known. The Home Office will place him or her in Section 4 Initial Asylum Support Accommodation, which is part of the Immigration and Asylum Act 1999, where he or she will have to share a bedroom with several others for a few weeks. The quality of the accommodation is usually awful. Asylum seekers are generally housed outside of London and the south east under the Home Office's dispersal policy, which was implemented to redistribute asylum seekers receiving state support around the UK and to prevent their concentration in the south east of England. However, only a quarter of local authorities participate in the scheme. The likelihood is that asylum seekers will be moved to one of the larger dispersal areas – Wakefield, Glasgow or Cardiff. Accommodation can only be provided in London in exceptional circumstances – for example, where hospital appointments are needed to treat a rare condition.

Adult asylum seekers are moved to a longer-stay unit after a few weeks. Conditions are better and, if they are lucky enough, a person may get their own room. They are given a money card ('Azure' card) that will be pre-loaded with less than £40 a week to pay for food, toiletries and clothing. Based on this low weekly amount, the poverty levels among asylum seekers are quite high. As a result, they are pushed into illegal working – or end up relying heavily on food banks and help from charities, including clothing and hardship funds for small amounts of cash for emergencies. This is very much a 'stuck' life. Access to adult learning is limited with few free classes available and full-time education denied to anyone over the age of 21. The formative years – when a young adult develops their sense of belonging in the world, completes their education, finds a job, has disposal income and starts a relationship – all lie in jeopardy.

Alas, the picture is one of despair, because life in Britain for young adult asylum seekers and refugees is very difficult – particularly for those in their twenties, who are often vulnerable, immature and have limited life experience because of disrupted childhoods and education. Many speak little English and struggle enormously. Admittedly, there will be some professional people who have been to university in their home countries, but these are a minority compared to the overall number of migrants in Britain. According to the British Red Cross, there are thousands of refugees and asylum seekers living in poverty in the UK.

The definition of poverty given by the Joseph Rowntree Foundation (Goulden and D'Arcy, 2014, p 3) is: *'When a person's resources (mainly their material resources) are not sufficient to meet minimum needs (including social participation).'* The definition of destitution, as outlined in Section 95(3) of the Immigration and Asylum Act 1999, is as follows.

*A person is destitute if he does not have adequate accommodation or any means of obtaining it (whether or not his other essential living needs are met); or he has adequate accommodation or the means of obtaining it, but cannot meet his other essential living needs.*

A destitution test is carried out by the Home Office to determine whether a person is 'destitute' because they do not have adequate accommodation or enough money to meet their living expenses and those of any dependents, either at the present time or within the next 14 days. Less than £40 a week is the level of cash support provided. This is significantly lower than income support levels and is not increased every year. Strategies to tackle poverty for refugees and asylum seekers have been limited and partial. The issue has never been pushed to the top of any government agenda or seen as a priority.

It is not only new arrivals who are presented with this awful life while their asylum application is being processed. Young asylum seekers who were formerly UASC, and were age assessed to be over the age of 18, also end up in this position. Many care leavers, too, who reach ARE and have had unsuccessful Human Rights Assessments will end up with minimum Home Office support. Unless they can lodge a fresh claim or request a judicial review, they could end up under Section 4 Home Office support, provided they agree to voluntarily return to their country of origin. Very few people agree to this and those who do are placed in multi-shared accommodation like new arrivals (Initial Asylum Support Accommodation). They are provided with minimal financial assistance, which for some inexplicable reason is a couple of pounds less than what new arrivals receive.

The frank picture of asylum is that unless somebody gets their initial five years LTR, they end up with a totally miserable existence here in Britain. Waiting to secure refugee status can take several years and, often, people must be prepared to endure several setbacks. It can take two or more years for an adult asylum seeker to be asked to attend a substantive interview. A decision may then be given within 6 to 12 months. If unsuccessful, the appeal process can take up to 18 months or longer. The decision-making process is like that of UASC and care leavers, in the sense that it is hard to pinpoint why the delays are excessive and/or why some receive status and others don't, irrespective of how similar their circumstances might be. It is estimated that two-thirds are initially turned down, but up to 60 per cent of those are successful upon appeal.

Very little education is offered to adult asylum seekers, except perhaps for free ESOL lessons once a week, because of a lack of suitable courses and cost implications. A small number, though, are successful in getting financial support by applying for grants via charitable organisations, but this is mainly for those fluent in English, who have good literacy skills and academic potential. Unlike UASC and care leavers, adult asylum seekers struggle with bureaucracy and even those who are successful and get refugee status often find completing a CV or applying for Universal Credit very difficult to do by themselves.

Mental health issues among adult asylum seekers are very high. Many have mentioned that their emotional health is far worse here than back home. PTSD, depression and suicidal thoughts are the most common, but psychotic behaviour has also been noted in some. Access to support is limited. They can be offered 12 sessions of talking therapy, but are sometimes refused if their emotional health is considered complex and high need, with the vast majority falling within this remit. Psychologists have stated that offering 12 sessions could result in unpicking problems that will make matters worse – and therefore, more often than not, no therapy sessions take place.

Even if young adults are given refugee status, they are still at risk of becoming homeless because they are given only 28 days to vacate the Home Office asylum accommodation and find a means of supporting themselves, otherwise they are evicted. Very few can find anywhere during this short timeframe, not least because private landlords request a deposit and rent in advance. With regard to applying for benefits, including housing benefit under Universal Credit, there is insufficient time to process the application before a person must leave their accommodation. Motivation, resilience and sheer willpower are needed to sustain this difficult predicament. Even those who eventually get their refugee status and manage to find accommodation are often faced with low-paid employment and a chronic housing shortage for their long-term future. Often, they will struggle to get social housing with a void in information being supplied to them about applications, the bidding system and council tax. Their rights, under international law, to be placed high on the social housing list is mainly ignored, which results in most people living in poor-quality rented shared accommodation in deprived areas.

## The poverty trap

Whether somebody stays in Home Office asylum accommodation or they leave to stay with a friend, they will encounter great hardship while their claim for asylum is being processed. Living on less than £40 a week places enormous toll on the person and affects both their physical and mental well-being. The biggest campaign in the UK at present is for the lifting of the ban that prevents asylum seekers from working. Lobbying for this is mainly done through charitable organisations such as the British Red Cross, the Refugee Council and Migrants Organise.

Those who reside in Home Office asylum accommodation are given 21 days' notice to vacate if they reach ARE status. Although some may have intentions or are in the process of lodging a fresh application for asylum, this process is not immediate and therefore leaves the individual with no option but to go and sofa surf with friends. Some also turn to charitable organisations to help them find a room. Isolation and boredom are huge issues for adult asylum seekers, with many having to endure life with little means of entertainment or stimulus, including access to a television or laptop.

Statistics are unclear, but it is roughly estimated that one out of six adult asylum seekers vanish if their application for asylum is refused. Those who are unsuccessful with their first application and have had a fresh claim accepted are sometimes allowed to return under Section 4 Home Office accommodation – or if they can prove they are going through all the possible changes to leave the UK, including signing up for the

Assisted Voluntary Return or being in touch with their embassy for emergency travel documents.

Asylum seekers who reach ARE and who are given notice to leave their Section 4 accommodation are given food vouchers to the value of less than £40 per week, which, once again, renders them reliant on charitable donations and food banks. They are also required to report to the Home Office at Lunar House in Croydon. This places them in a very difficult situation. They do not have funds to travel, for example, from Kent or East Sussex or Bedfordshire, and they are not given travel warrants. Once again, they turn to charitable organisations, their mosque or church for help. Others who, with help from advocate agencies, have confronted the Home Office about this absurdity in asking people with such limited means to report as often as fortnightly have had various degrees of success – either the reporting instructions have been reduced or they have been provided with travel warrants. Another fear faced by asylum seekers during reporting at Lunar House is the prospect of getting arrested and put in a detention centre – which appears to be done at random and based on vacancies in detention centres, even in cases where the individual has made a fresh claim for asylum.

# Deportation Orders and detention

A Deportation Order under UK immigration law allows for someone over the age of 17 to be removed from the UK, but it also means they can be kept in custody until they are deported. A Deportation Order, which is made on the orders of an immigration official as opposed to a court, means a person may be held in detention without any warning. However, this rarely happens to anybody aged between 17 and 19. It occurs mainly after applications for asylum are refused or ARE is reached upon unsuccessful appeals, when the Home Office thinks the person might try to avoid it, or if asylum seekers/refugees have been convicted of a crime that carries a prison sentence. In addition to refused asylum seekers, detention centres also include visa overstayers and foreign national offenders who are being deported after serving prison sentences.

On average, 24,000 people per year are held at some point in one of the seven detention centres in the UK. Each has the capacity to hold up to 3000 detainees at any one time. The majority stay less than two months, although the UK is the only country in Europe that does not have a time limit on how long somebody should be detained. Approximately 40 per cent (on average two out of five) will be deported, while the rest will be released back into the community – for example, if an asylum seeker successfully lodges a fresh application, which will have meant their time in incarceration served no purpose (as I experienced with a young person I previously worked with).

In my role as a social worker, I visited a young man in a detention centre who had served a Detention and Training Order in a Young Offenders Institute (YOI). He was taken to the immigration removal centre after he had completed the custodial part of his sentence. This young person only had UASC leave up until he was 17-and-a-half and had failed to lodge a further application to get this extended prior to his imprisonment. The Home Office was advised by the YOI of his criminal conviction and he was subsequently issued a deportation order.

One thing I learned during this time is that prison staff know little about asylum matters and, unless the Refugee Council are contacted to help (which in this case they weren't), little assistance can or will be given without securing legal support through an immigration solicitor. Had this young person been given access to a solicitor, he would have been given help to make a fresh application for asylum. If this had been done, this may have prevented the Home Office issuing him with a deportation order. In turn, he would have been spared a wasted year of his life held in an overcrowded detention centre before eventually getting released once a fresh asylum application was made. The young person achieved this thanks to the advocacy service, which was attached to the detention centre. They put him in contact with an immigration solicitor who took on his case.

His release from custody, however, brought little happiness or certainty. While in detention, his local authority carried out a Human Rights Assessment that resulted in a negative outcome. Owing to his Deportation Order, they withdrew his leaving care entitlement and closed the case. After he successfully lodged a fresh claim for asylum, his release from detention only came when an older friend agreed he could live with him. The young person in question thereafter only received the bare minimum government financial assistance for adult asylum seekers. He was released from detention, but the 18plus team did not re-open the case despite legal intervention requesting a review of his circumstances. His only practical help thereafter was through charitable organisations.

This young man's story is indicative of so many others and shows how easy it is for somebody like him to get lost and forgotten about in the system. Changeover between teams, having several different workers, imprisonment and an overall lack of consistency and specialist help adds weight to somebody going deeper into a downward spiral.

Detention centres present differently to prisons in the sense that some restrictions are relaxed – eg detainees can have their own mobile phone and are allowed to wear their own clothes. However, being held in prison-like conditions, without a time constraint, causes a lot of anxiety and distress and is psychologically damaging. An undercover investigation into Tinley House, a detention centre at Gatwick Airport, by the BBC's *Panorama* programme in 2017 (which coincidently was where my client was sent) exposed the centre as short-staffed and having poorly trained officers. Violence often erupted among the under-occupied and bored detainees were given little to do and did not have access to any form of education or mental stimulus. It showed detainees being abused and humiliated. Self-harming and drug-taking was rife. Detainees of all ages were made to share cells and thefts among detainees were commonplace. The programme concluded that privacy, dignity or any form of peacefulness were virtually impossible to achieve.

# Conclusion

This chapter has summed up how difficult is it for any adult asylum seeker who comes to the UK to rebuild their lives. Obstacles are placed in their way from the moment they set foot on British soil. They may be safe from the harm they left behind, but a different type of life challenge awaits them. A national crisis in the UK in 2020 added to the list of difficulties already being endured by refugees and asylum seekers with the arrival of the coronavirus, which has brought additional hardship and suffering. A large majority of people in low-paid employment lost their jobs and few were in a position to be furloughed. It was a time of loneliness, isolation and fear, and while many are accustomed to dealing with crises and hardship, life in the UK became even harder than prior to the arrival of COVID-19. Charitable organisations were flooded with hardship requests. Face-to-face contact was carried out by charities such as the British Red Cross, who delivered basic essentials including food parcels, hygiene packs, mobile phone top-ups and hardship funds to where people were staying.

# Chapter 9 | Leaving nobody behind

## Introduction

The sad truth is that people have always been left behind. When it comes to the asylum story, there is no such thing as a clean story where every loose end gets tidied up before its completion. This chapter looks at the large number of displaced people in the Middle East and all across Africa, where there is little hope of the problem getting sorted. Instead, it is feared that the problem will continue to intensify because the core roots of war, tyranny and poverty are not being addressed or rectified.

Throughout this book, you have been told stories of bravery, courage and resilience. Equally, you have seen glimpses of heartache, misery and suffering. You have also witnessed the fighting spirit, determination and spiritual strength of young people. In many ways, young people appear to be much kinder and morally attuned than the officials who deal with their asylum claims. Only too often, the bureaucratic world sees the person as a client first and human being second. Take, for example, the current family reunification arrangements for UASC in the UK. If, for a moment, professionals were genuinely empathic and compassionate, and able to imagine themselves in the position of the young people or their parents, then a major shift in this present deadlock could be made.

## Global displacement and resettlement

The number of displaced people across the world stands at over 70 million people and reaches across most of Africa, the Middle East and South America. Interestingly, there are several countries in the world where people leave to seek asylum, while other citizens remain displaced in their country. Some of these countries that people flee from are blighted by war, famine and persecution, yet they accept refugees from neighbouring countries – making the subject of asylum even harder to analyse. For example, South Sudan – which has the largest refugee crisis in Africa and the third largest in the world – has seen 2.3 million of its people flee to neighbouring countries, including Kenya, while approximately 1.8 million remain internally displaced. In Somalia, over 300,000 have fled the country, while the number of displaced citizens stands at 2.6 million people. A similar number have left Ethiopia, where over a million are estimated to be internally displaced. However, Ethiopia is home to the second largest refugee population in Africa after Uganda, with refugees mainly coming from

South Sudan, Somalia and Eritrea, although most of these live in camps with poor conditions.

The Middle East paints a similar picture. While over 3 million people have fled Yemen in recent years, there remains over 2.3 million who are internally displaced and who live in squalid camp conditions. After four decades of war and conflict, Afghanistan already has one of the world's largest refugee populations. This has resulted in millions seeking refuge in various parts of the world – mainly in Pakistan, Iran and Europe – while 1.2 million remain internally displaced. While many Kurds in the Kurdistan Duhok region in Northern Iraq have fled to neighbouring countries, also in their millions, there is still over a million displaced people living in camps there, consisting of local Kurds and other Kurds who have fled the war in Syria.

Global resettlement is an ambitious plan whereby countries around the world agree to take in an annual agreed number of refugees, sufficient to reduce the vast number of people displaced across the globe in inhumane and unsafe camp conditions. However, would the UK agreeing to this safe passage of entry change, in any way, the harsh living existence that spontaneous arrivals face? Or would they, too, come to an under-class existence coupled with entrenched and untreated trauma? Are they going to feel abandoned after they arrive here and experience danger in new and unfamiliar ways?

Currently, success stories are few and far between, but these mainly stem from young people who came to the UK under resettlement schemes. They have the added pro-tection of being given refugee status and don't have to endure the stress and re-traumatised angst of waiting for a decision on their legal status. Basically, from the moment they arrive, they can start rebuilding their lives. It is in this group of young people – and not the spontaneous arrivals – that you will mainly find those who end up going to university and go on into professional careers. The prime advantage of resettlement schemes ensures that, prior to arrival, the specific needs of the young people are known and the correct support is put into place, including trained foster carers who await their arrival.

Charities and lobbying bodies have often campaigned that it is a false economy when the government only allows small numbers to enter under resettlement schemes (managed migration), as seen previously under the Dubs Agreement. This initially meant that the UK would allow 3000 Syrian refugees into the country; but they backtracked on their promise, resulting in only 480 eventually being allowed to come. Most asylum seekers coming to the UK are spontaneous arrivals at ports – both UASC and adults. Organisations like Safe Passage are working with the government in the hope that the UK will take up to 5000 children and adults a year from conflict zones in the Middle East and Africa under a new global resettlement scheme. However, while emphasis will be on such resettlement programmes in the future, the crisis in parts of Europe remains. For example, there are still over 4000 displaced children living in camps in Greece (a quarter of whom are believed to be sex trafficked). In addition to this, over 7000 children have gone missing in Italy since 2018 – many are also believed to have been sex trafficked.

# The Dublin Regulation and family reunification

Currently, young people are not allowed to sponsor their parents to come to the UK. The irony is that this is not allowed under UK law, but is allowed under EU law. The Dublin Regulation is a part of European law that allows the transfer of asylum cases from one European country to another. It dictates that those arriving in their first country of safety must apply for asylum in that country, but this has not been adhered to. The fiascos of the immigration system in Italy, Spain and Greece meant that records were either not maintained or the system became overburdened by the large numbers. The Dublin Regulation means that if a young person in a European country has an older sibling (over the age of 18), parent, aunt, uncle or grandparent resident in the UK, then they are eligible to seek reunification with that family member. In the case of UASC, they can apply to be transferred to another EU country (where they have a relative) to have their claim processed, but this is mainly ignored. The potential for young people to reunite with their families down the line, after they get permanent residency in the UK, is little consolation because at that point they will be adults who have lost out on their childhood years.

Social workers and 18plus advisers rarely discuss family reunification with young people because they either know little about the process or they know the cost implications may be a deterrent for the local authority. There is also little discussion in the media about this topic. There were thousands of children in the Calais camps and in the 'camps' in Greece who then came to the UK as UASC but were not allowed to seek reunification with their families. And nobody spoke out on their behalf. There was no lobbying. In fact, there appears to be an anti-lobby towards family reunification in the UK – in fear of sowing a seed that might open the floodgates?

A lack of insight and empathy means that young people are expected to live lives without family members who could easily be allowed to come to the UK if the system and legal aid funding supported it. If this was in place though, it would help greatly in driving young people forward and doing well in education. Instead, they must contend with limited and sometimes no information about family members. These factors impact greatly on mental health and many worry about their siblings' lost years and growing up without them. Now there is little chance of anybody having hope of reunion.

I was told about a handful of cases relating to young adults who had obtained UK citizenship and requested help from the local authority to sponsor the arrival of younger siblings from Europe. In one case, a young man (20) had agreed for his brother (14) to join him from Austria. The local authority carried out a short assessment on the suitability of accommodation and the welfare of the young man who was suffering from PTSD. They assessed him as a suitable carer, despite his lingering mental health concerns. However, the local authority was unaware that his brother had endured sexual exploitation in Austria and, when he arrived in the UK, the older brother struggled to take care of his brother, who was suffering trauma and flashbacks. The toll of his brother's emotional fragility and his own needs meant that the placement soon broke down.

If better assessment, planning and aftercare had been put into this case, an entirely different outcome could have occurred. A lack of aftercare and 'family' work means that the older brother was left supporting his younger brother without the skills needed to look after a younger sibling. But I was told this is not unusual and, despite the low numbers involved in family reunification, a large percentage – up to 80 per cent – break down owing to money or issues with accommodation.

Currently, EU legislation states that reunification should take place as soon as possible and there is a three-month timescale in place. Often, it is found that these timescales are stretched to the maximum or sometimes breached, but alas few cases are legally challenged because of funding. Furthermore, many professionals feel that immigration officials simply don't care if a young person remains in a squat in Athens, even if they do have a close relative in the UK who is willing to sponsor them. This policy might change post-Brexit, but it is thought that Britain cannot expect to transfer out (deport) unless it is willing to accept referrals into the UK from European countries.

# Moral duty

It is often questioned if Britain has a moral duty to be doing more for asylum seekers – both now and in the future. Is there a need for a call for empathy and kindness, given that asylum seekers are among the most vulnerable in the UK? Is a call for conscience needed in the government and Home Office? They must know that the current provisions in place for adult asylum seekers are inadequate and unjust, and barely allow for existence. Sadly, the common answer to all of these questions relates back to government and its control of finances, along with a fear of the general public thinking they are treating asylum seekers better than citizens from the lower socio-economic classes. For meaningful progress to occur, there would have to be key changes implemented, including the following.

» Changes in policies/legislation on the resettlement of children in Europe from conflict zones. Every year, the UK should take a minimum of 1000 children and young people and offer them sanctuary under specially designed resettlement programmes. They also need to be given automatic refugee status in order to settle and rebuild their lives.

» Organisations like Safe Passage and others who champion refugees' rights to legal entry to the UK should be better supported. In doing so, this will greatly enhance the chances of young people being brought here by means of safe and legal routes – as opposed to spontaneous arrivals whereby young people risk their lives in many dangerous ways.

» Emphasis should be placed on family reunification and efforts should be made to ensure that it is a possibility for the majority and not the minority, like it currently stands. Common sense, empathy and compassion need to be pushed to the top of the agenda, with recognition given to mental well-being and the impact that family separation has on people.

» More honesty and transparency are required by the government, which sometimes lends to misinformation – ie it is doing a lot to help young asylum seekers and refugees. This is not true and if it appears to be the case, it is superficial and by default, given the hostile environment it has created. If the numbers of spontaneous arrivals are matched against those who come under resettlement schemes, it is easily determined that the largest number by far are spontaneous arrivals and it is these who endure the hardest system.

In addition to these proposed changes, it is felt that a shift in public opinion is needed (including that of the government, too). All too often the general belief is that young asylum seekers flock to Britain because of some type of 'Nirvana' dream. The truth is, young asylum seekers are often pushed into coming here as a last resort, after being forced out of other countries (Italy, France and Belgium) by police, sometimes using tear gas. Many arrive in Britain without a clue about the country. A few might have heard about Manchester United or know that the Queen lives here. Some are advised to come here after having been wrongly age assessed in another European country, even though it is often visibly evident that they are still under the age of 18. They arrive here exhausted and at the point where they will go anywhere in order to settle and start a new life.

If there is any hope of the circumstances of asylum seekers changing in the future, there are key areas that need proper funding and investment. These first steps towards a better system in the UK will undoubtedly lead to lessening the social divide and promote integration; they include the following.

>> The weekly money allowance, under Section 95, needs to be increased and to be at least on par with benefit recipients. Financial support should also be given for clothing and footwear. People should not be expected to look towards charities for this help.

>> Asylum seekers should be allowed to work and earn their money. The vast majority want to work and in doing so there would be a massive boost to the economy. This would also help enormously with their mental health.

>> Accommodation of all kinds needs massive improvement. Instead of providing overcrowded and damp accommodation that is not fit for purpose, humane and decent housing needs to be provided to help assist in rebuilding lives and in the treating of trauma.

>> Proper educational opportunities should be made available. This includes vocational courses and re-training programmes for doctors, nurses and teachers, of which there is a current shortage here in the UK. Without financial assistance for both, there can be no shift, because few charitable bodies can give grants that would cover the cost of these courses. The expense would, however, be worth it in the end. Many asylum seekers were trained professionals in their own countries.

# Conclusion

Claiming asylum may be no different to what we have now, with those seeking safety in Britain coming from the same countries with the same problems. The war in the Middle East is enduring, with an uncertain future. The conflict and poverty in Africa are also enduring. Then there is always the possibility of further global conflict in several 'hot' spots in the world, including Russia, Latvia, China, Taiwan, the Persian Gulf, Kashmir, Israel and North Korea. The simple fact is that anywhere in the world has the potential for war – even Britain. Irrespective of where there is war and suffering in the world, asylum seekers will continue to come to Britain in the hope of a better life.

When I questioned whether services for asylum seekers had improved in the UK over the past 20 years, this resulted in professionals mainly saying they hadn't. Long waiting lists for asylum decisions remain, and poor housing and limited opportunities were the same two decades ago. While the system has become more used to dealing with asylum seekers and has greater general knowledge of their circumstances than previous generations, this is not backed up with resources or investment.

Although some charitable organisations do sterling lobbying and championing for change, there appears to be silence from statutory bodies. The simple truth is that if change does not occur and if resources do not increase, then fear, shame, destitution, isolation, exploitation, poor health, discrimination and injustice will remain as core elements in the current generation of asylum seekers and those who seek safe shelter in the Britain of the future.

# Glossary

This glossary contains many of the key words used within the professional arena of asylum to describe the main legal terms and processes. It is not designed to be a definitive list, but it covers the main nomenclature and definitions used when describing young asylum seekers and refugees who seek asylum in the UK. These have been gathered from a wide range of sources, including my own definitions, but many have come from the UNHCR glossary of terms.

**Appeal Rights Exhausted (ARE):** a person whose request for asylum was refused, and who has made all the appeals they can, without any success.

**Assisted Voluntary Return:** a UK scheme, operated by the Home Office, to help people return permanently to their home country.

**Assisted Voluntary Return and Reintegration:** administrative, logistical or financial support, including reintegration assistance, to migrants unable or unwilling to remain in the host country or country of transit and who decide to return to their country of origin.

**Asylum:** the grant, by a state, of protection on its territory to persons from another state who are fleeing persecution or serious danger. Asylum encompasses various elements, including not forcing asylum seekers to return to a country in which they are liable to be subjected to persecution, but to grant permission to remain on the territory of the asylum country and give humane standards of treatment.

**Asylum seeker:** the legal term for somebody who has applied to stay in the UK on the grounds that if they were to return to their country of origin, their lives would be in danger.

**Biometrics Residence Permit (BRP):** a form of ID when someone applies to settle in the UK. It contains a photograph, name, place of birth, whether the person has recourse to public funds and details of any status and conditions of stay.

**British citizenship:** when someone lives and works in the UK, free of any immigration controls.

**Care leaver:** a young person who was previously Looked After and has now left the care system.

**Children Act 1989:** the core piece of legislation that serves as the legal framework for all children's social care responsibilities in the UK.

**Children and Social Work Act 2017:** a recent piece of legislation that introduces new duties to care leavers, including the need for a Local Offer and the requirement to work with someone until they turn 25 – whether in education or not.

**Corporate parent:** an organisation that fulfils the role of parent.

**Country of origin:** refers to the country where a person ordinarily lives and where they had rights as a national from birth.

**Displacement:** the movement of persons who have been forced or obliged to flee or to leave their homes or places of habitual residence, in particular as a result of or in order to avoid the effects of armed conflict, situations of generalized violence, violations of human rights or natural or human-made disasters.

**Dublin Regulation:** an EU law that designates member state responsibility for examining an asylum application. Its purpose is to assign one member state to one asylum seeker to ensure that individuals do not ask for asylum in multiple countries, and that governments do not outright ignore a person's asylum request.

**Dubs Agreement:** relates to Section 67 of the Immigration Act 2016 (the Dubs Amendment) and requires the government to decide 'as soon as possible' after the passing of the Immigration Act 2016 to relocate and support unaccompanied refugee children from Europe.

**Economic migrants:** persons who leave their countries purely for economic reasons unrelated to the refugee definition, or in order to seek material improvements in their livelihood. Economic migrants do not fall within the criteria for refugee status and are therefore not entitled to benefit from international protection.

**ESOL:** English for Speakers of Other Languages. A course mainly used in the UK to help students from all over the world to become fluent in spoken and written English.

**Family reunification:** the right of non-nationals to enter and reside in a country where their family members reside lawfully or of which they have the nationality in order to preserve the family unit.

**First Tier Tribunal:** when an asylum claim is refused with the right to appeal, the appeal is brought to the First Tier Tribunal in the first instance.

**Home Office:** the government department responsible for managing immigration into the UK.

**Human Rights:** individual protections for a safe and decent life as laid out in the Human Rights Act 1998, including Article 2 (Right to life), Article 3 (Freedom from inhuman and degrading treatment/torture) and Article 8 (Right to family life).

**Human Rights Assessment (HRA):** an assessment that is carried out to establish whether a young person who is Appeals Rights Exhausted is eligible for three months' Home Office support based on Article 3 and 8, ECHR. Individual local authorities are responsible for conducting this assessment.

**Humanitarian protection:** given (initially for five years) to those who are refused refugee status following their Home Office substantive interview, but thought to be at risk of persecution or death if they returned to their country of origin. Those granted are entitled to similar rights to resident British nationals.

**Independent Reviewing Officer (IRO):** an individual responsible for ensuring the work done by social care professionals is of a high standard and helps someone's life progress according to plan. They also chair Looked After Child (LAC) reviews.

**Integration:** the two-way process of mutual adaptation between migrants and the societies in which they live – ie whereby migrants are incorporated into the social, economic, cultural and political life of the receiving community.

**Leave to Remain:** a catch-all term for those given an initial five years to stay in the UK – ie granted refugee status or humanitarian protection by the Home Office.

**Leaving Care Service:** the main service that works with asylum seekers after they turn 18.

**Looked After Child (LAC) review:** a meeting chaired by the Independent Reviewing Officer (IRO), which gathers together all the relevant professionals, the foster carer and the Looked After Child to review general progress.

**Modern slavery:** the recruitment, movement, harbouring or receiving of children, women or men using force, coercion, abuse of vulnerability, deception or using other methods for the purpose of exploitation. See also Trafficking.

**Naturalisation:** the process of somebody becoming a British national (those granted refugee status and humanitarian protection) are eligible to apply.

**Negative decision:** somebody who has lodged an application with the Home Office and has been refused asylum – either refugee status or humanitarian protection – following their substantive interview.

**No Recourse to Public Funds:** not being allowed to make use of resources or services that originate from tax money including all forms of benefits (including Universal Credit, which incorporates Housing Benefit). People who have failed asylum claims fall into this category.

**Overstayer:** somebody who has been refused asylum by the Home Office and who has reached the stage of All Rights Exhausted in the appeals, process but remains in the UK despite no legal status and having No Recourse to Public Funds.

**Personal adviser:** an allocated worker and primary contact for those who have turned 18; a person who should be the first point of contact when support is needed.

**Personal Education Plan (PEP):** a plan drawn up between an individual, worker and, usually, a college or sixth-form tutor, which sets out specific, achievable education targets.

**Positive decision:** somebody who has applied for asylum and been granted Leave to Remain status.

**Post-traumatic stress disorder (PTSD):** a mental health condition where somebody has witnessed death, near death, serious injury, extreme violence, fear or extreme distress and exhibits symptoms that affects their ability to function in everyday life as a result of flashbacks.

**Refugee:** a person who *'owing to a well-founded fear of being persecuted for reasons of race, religion, nationality, membership of a particular social group, or political opinion, is outside the country of his nationality, and is unable to or, owing to such fear, is unwilling to avail himself of the protection of that country'* (Definition quoted from the 1951 Refugee Convention).

**Refugee status:** given (initially for five years) to those who have had successful asylum claims following their Home Office substantive interview. Those granted are entitled to similar rights to resident British nationals.

**Refugee with Leave:** a person who has claimed asylum in the UK and been given 'Leave to Remain', which gives them similar rights to resident nationals.

**Refused asylum seeker:** a legal term for people who applied for asylum, but have received a negative decision, which could mean them having to leave the country.

**Resettlement:** the transfer of refugees from the country in which they have sought asylum to another state that has agreed to admit them. The refugees will usually be granted asylum or some other form of long-term resident rights and, in many cases, will have the opportunity to become naturalised citizens. For this reason, resettlement is a durable solution and is a tool for the protection of refugees. It is also a practical example of international burden and responsibility sharing.

**Separated children:** children, as defined in Article 1 of the United Nations Convention on the Rights of the Child, who have been separated from both parents, or from their previous legal or customary primary caregiver, but not necessarily from other relatives. These may, therefore, include children accompanied by other adult family members.

**Smuggling:** people (smugglers) who smuggle those who want help to cross borders and whose activities are secret, illegal and done to make profit.

**Stateless persons:** persons who are not considered as nationals by any state under the operation of its law, including persons whose nationality is not established.

**Statement of Evidence (SEF):** each UASC young person needs to complete an SEF within 60 days of their initial claim for asylum, to explain why they are claiming asylum.

**Substantive interview:** the main Home Office interview where people attend, are interviewed and given the opportunity to state why they are claiming asylum in the UK.

**Trafficking:** traffickers buy and sell people and 'own' them. They move people within countries and across international borders to exploit vulnerable people for labour, sex, benefits fraud and for the sale of human organs.

**UASC leave:** a child under the age of 17½ who has applied for asylum but been refused refugee status and humanitarian protection will be granted a form of limited leave if there are no adequate reception arrangements in the country to which they would be returned.

**Unaccompanied:** children under the age of 18 who are here without a parent or responsible adult who is accountable for their welfare, safeguarding and development.

**Unaccompanied asylum-seeking child (UASC):** children who have applied for asylum, who are outside their country of origin and are separated from both parents, or previous/legal customary primary caregiver.

**Undocumented:** somebody without papers that confirm they are legally entitled to be in the country; however, it does not necessarily mean they are illegally in the country.

**Upper Tier Tribunal:** if an initial appeal is dismissed, with the right to a further appeal, this appeal is brought to the Upper Tier Tribunal.

**Voluntary repartition:** return to the country of origin based on the refugee's free and informed decision.

# Useful contacts

Here is a list of some key organisations in the UK and Ireland that lend support and guidance to asylum seekers and refugees. They are mainly the better-known organisations, many of which are national or London based. This list is by no means exhaustive and should not deter anybody from seeking further information or support from their nearest local organisation – details of which can be found using Google to search the local area or by asking the larger organisations (such as the Refugee Council or the British Red Cross) for details of their nearest branch.

**The Refugee Council** is a national UK charitable organisation. They seek to address laws, policy and government guidance that are often unsympathetic to refugees, complicated and unfair. They provide specialist help to refugees and people seeking asylum and have an in-depth understanding of the needs and challenges they face. They also carry out research, policy and advocacy for refugees and work with decision-makers to create and influence policy.

> **The Refugee Council**
> PO Box 68614
> London, E15 1NS
> **Telephone**: 0207 346 6700
> **Email**: info@refugeecouncil.org.uk
> **Website**: www.refugeecouncil.org.uk

**The British Red Cross** supports vulnerable refugees and asylum seekers. They provide refugee services in 58 towns and cities across the country, offering care and support when people arrive in the UK after a political or humanitarian crisis. They also run a family tracing service for those who have been separated from their family and are unaware of their whereabouts.

> **The British Red Cross**
> London Office
> 44 Moorfields
> London, EC2Y 9AL
> **Telephone**: 0344 871 11 11
> **Email**: contactus@redcross.org.uk
> **Website**: www.redcross.org.uk

**Coram Children's Legal Centre** – part of the Coram group of charities – promotes and protects the rights of children in the UK and internationally, in line with the UN Convention on the Rights of the Child. Experts in all areas of children's rights, immigration, child protection, education and juvenile justice, they also provide legal advice and representation, carry out research and produce evidence informing law, policy, practice and system reform.

### Coram Children's Legal Centre
Coram Campus
41 Brunswick Square
London, WC1N 1AZ
**Telephone**: 0207 520 0300
**Email**: info@coramclc.org.uk
**Website**: www.coram.org.uk

**Safe Passage** helps thousands of unaccompanied child refugees each year who arrive in Europe in search of safety. They work directly with children who may be stuck in squalid camps or sleeping rough on city streets unaware of their legal right to travel safely through Europe. In addition to helping child refugees access their rights, they also work closely with the government on resettlement programmes for young asylum seekers into Britain.

### Safe Passage
136 Cavell Street
Whitechapel
London, E1 2JΛ
**Telephone**: 0208 017 2937
**Email**: info@safepassage.org.uk
**Website**: www.safepassage.org.uk

**Together with Migrant Children** works with children, young people and families who are migrants, refugees or asylum seekers. They work nationwide, with the majority of their work in London and the south east. They provide holistic support for families, support with safeguarding, work and advocacy with families with No Recourse to Public Funds and carry out assessment work for a wide variety of purposes.

### Together with Migrant Children
Wolvercote Young People's Centre
Oxford, OX2 8AU
**Telephone**: 01865 528 658
**Email**: hello@togethermigrantchildren.org.uk
**Website**: www.togethermigrantchildren.org.uk

**Migrant Help** assist those seeking asylum in the UK with applying for accommodation and financial support, reporting issues with asylum accommodation, and any other advice needed during their asylum journey. They provide support during the post-decision period, whether the decision has been positive or negative. They also provide specialist support and accommodation to victims of human trafficking and modern slavery, and their dependants.

**Migrant Help**
Charlton House
Dour Street
Dover, CT16 1AT
**Telephone**: 01304 203977
**Email**: info@migranthelpuk.org
**Website**: www.migranthelpuk.org

**Migrants Organise** is a lobbying charity that empowers refugees and migrants campaign for power, dignity and justice. They develop leadership and open up spaces for relational, organised participation of migrants and refugees in public life. Other services include training and preparing people to tell their life stories. They also speak in oral evidence sessions in parliament as well as sharing stories in the media.

**Migrants Organise**
2 Thorpe Close
London, W10 5XL
**Telephone**: 020 8964 4815
**Email**: info@migrantsorganise.org
**Website**: www.migrantsorganise.org

**Community Action for Refugees and Asylum Seekers (CARAS)** is a London charity that offers a wide range of group activities to support people of all ages to develop their English skills, access services and opportunities, build supportive social networks and to feel welcomed. They work with individuals to make sure they receive the specific support that matches their situation, no matter how complex.

**CARAS**
25 Blakenham Road
London, SW17 8NE
**Telephone**: 0208 767 5378
**Email**: info@caras.org.uk
**Website**: www.caras.org.uk

**Asylum Welcome** tackle suffering and isolation among asylum seekers, refugees and detainees who have fled persecution and danger in their own countries, and seek refuge in Oxford and Oxfordshire. They assist asylum seekers who are homeless and destitute, as well as being a referral service to other organisations, responding to urgent health needs and brokering urgent communication with the Home Office.

**Asylum Welcome**
Unit 7, Newtec Place
Magdalen Road
Oxford, OX4 1RE
**Telephone**: 01865 722082
**Email**: advice@asylum-welcome.org
**Website**: www.asylum-welcome.org

**Kent Refugee Action Network (KRAN)** is a Kent-based charity that supports unaccompanied young refugees – aged 11 to 24 years – living in the community. They provide education, mentoring and befriending and drop-in services to facilitate greater cohesion and to enable young refugees to live fulfilled and independent lives.

**KRAN**
Unit 1
34 Simmonds Road
Wincheap Industrial Estate
Canterbury, CT1 3RA
**Telephone**: 01227 634320
**Email**: via website
**Website**: www.kran.org.uk

**Dost Centre for Young Refugees and Migrants** is a one-stop charitable organisation based in East London. It aims to improve the quality of life for children and young people – aged between 11 and 25 – with refugee and asylum-seeking backgrounds, as well as those who have been trafficked and are undocumented. They carry out a diverse youth and education programme with young people and provide psychological casework if required.

**Dost**
Newham Leisure Centre
281 Prince Regent Lane
London, E13 8SD
**Telephone**: 07852 955711
**Email**: marian@dostcentre.co.uk
**Website**: www.dostcentre.co.uk

**Refugee Support Network (RSN)** helps young refugees and survivors of trafficking to build more hopeful futures through education. They provide a range of services which help 15–25 year-olds seeking safety in the UK to get into, stay in and do well in education. They recruit and train community volunteers to provide bespoke one-to-one educational mentoring – a blend of EAL tutoring and well-being support – to young people in their area across London, Oxford, Birmingham and the East of England.

**RSN**
1st Floor
The Salvation Army Building
32 Manor Park Rd
London, NW10 4JJ
**Telephone**: email contact only
**Email**: via website
**Website**: www.refugeesupportnetwork.org

**Consonant** (formerly Asylum Aid and Migrants Resource Centre) is a London-based charity that supports and advises migrants, including those in need of protection, in the UK. They seek to ensure that migrants are empowered to offer their skills, energy and resources to British society. They provide legal advice to migrants, refugees and asylum seekers, as well as free English language courses, computer classes and careers advice.

**Consonant**
Berol House
25 Ashley Road
London, N17 9LJ
**Telephone**: 0207 834 2505
**Email**: hello@consonant.org.uk
**Website**: www.consonant.org.uk

**Refugee Action** is a London-based charity that offers help and advice to refugees and asylum seekers on issues including the asylum process. They also help those struggling with poverty and homelessness and offer practical support and guidance for people who are resettling in the UK having fled conflict and persecution. They also provide resources to organisations working with refugees, asylum seekers and migrants across the UK.

**Refugee Action**
Victoria Charity Centre
11 Belgrave Road
London, SW1V 1RB
**Telephone**: 0808 8010 503
**Email**: info@refugee-action.org.uk
**Website**: www.refugee-action.org.uk

**Love146** is an international human rights organisation working to end child trafficking through prevention education and survivor care. They work in partnership with a wide range of statutory and non-statutory agencies involved in the immediate and ongoing needs of children and young people.

> **Love146**
> PO Box 51700
> London, SE8 9BX
> **Telephone:** 01845 6802146
> **Email:** info@love146.org.uk
> **Website:** www.love146.org.uk

**Student Action for Refugees (STAR)** is a national charity made up of over 30,000 students welcoming refugees to the UK. They volunteer at local refugee projects, campaign to improve the lives of refugees and educate people about refugees and asylum. STAR is made up of 50 groups from universities and colleges across the UK and a national team that co-ordinates and supports the groups.

> **STAR**
> Resource for London
> 356 Holloway Road
> London, N7 6PA
> **Telephone:** 0207 697 4130
> **Email:** via website
> **Website:** www.star-network.org.uk

**Freedom from Torture** is a medical foundation for the care of victims of torture. It provides specialist psychological therapy to help asylum seekers and refugees who have survived torture recover and rebuild their lives in the UK. With survivors, they campaign for change in the UK and across the world. They raise awareness and influence decision-makers about torture and its impact. They also provide training for professionals working with torture survivors.

> **Freedom from Torture**
> 111 Isledon Road
> London, N7 7JW
> **Telephone:** 020 7697 7777
> **Email:** via website
> **Website:** www.freedomfromtorture.org

**Refugees at Home** offers a helping hand and somewhere to stay at a time of crisis for asylum seekers over the age of 18 – many who have reached ARE and have lodged a fresh claim for asylum. They match refugees and asylum seekers who need a place to stay with people with a spare room in their homes.

**Refugees at Home**
21 Ballingdon Road
London, SW11 6AJ
**Telephone**: 0300 365 4724
**Email**: via website
**Website**: www.refugeesathome.org

**Detention Action** help support people held in immigration detention and to campaign for fundamental reform. They provide practical and emotional support to people who are detained at various UK detention centres, and people detained under immigration powers in London prisons. They are completely independent from the government and detention centres.

**Detention Action**
The Green House
244–254 Cambridge Heath Road
London, E2 9DA
**Telephone**: 0207 226 3114
**Email**: admin@detentionaction.org.uk
**Website**: www.detentionaction.org.uk

# Republic of Ireland

**The Irish Refugee Council** provide services and support for refugees and people seeking asylum in Ireland, as well as advocating for humane and dignified asylum procedures and responses to people fleeing persecution based on their sexual identity, religious beliefs, political stance, for protesting, for being female or for being an ethnic minority.

**The Irish Refugee Council**
37 Killarney Street
Mountjoy
Dublin 1, D01 NX74
**Telephone**: 00353 1 764 5854
**Email**: info@irishrefugeecouncil.ie
**Website**: www.irishrefugeecouncil.ie

**Spirasi** is the national centre for the rehabilitation of victims of torture in Ireland. Psychological support is available to individuals and families who have suffered cruel and inhumane or degrading treatment. It offers various psycho-social support, along with Medical Legal Reports (MLRs) for the protection process and English language classes for victims of torture and their families.

**Spirasi**
213 North Circular Road
Phibsborough
Dublin 7
**Telephone**: 01-8389664
**Email**: info@spirasi.ie
**Website**: www.spirasi.ie

# References/suggested reading

ADCS – The Association of Directors of Children's Services (2015) *Age Assessment Guidance.* [online] Available at: https://adcs.org.uk/safeguarding/article/age-assessment-information-sharing-for-unaccompanied-asylum-seeking-childre (accessed 17 July 2020).

Allocation of Accommodation Policy (2017) Home Office. [online] Available at: https://assets.publishing.service.gov.uk/government/uploads/system/uploads/attachment_data/file/597382/Allocation-Of-Accommodation-v5_0.pdf (accessed 17 July 2020).

Allsopp, J (2014) *Poverty Among Refugees and Asylum Seekers in the UK (An Evidence and Policy Review).* University of Birmingham (IRiS – Institute of Research into Superdiversity).

Alper, J and Howe, D (2013) *Assessing Adoptive and Foster Parents (Improving Analysis and Understanding of Parental Capacity).* Jessica Kingsley Publishers.

American Psychiatric Association (2013) *Diagnostic and Statistical Manual of Mental Disorders, Fifth Edition – DSM-5.* American Psychiatric Association.

APT and CEJIL (2008) Torture in International Law: A Guide to Jurisprudence. Association for the Prevention of Torture and the Centre for Justice and International Law. [online] Available at: www.apt.ch/sites/default/files/publications/jurisprudenceguide.pdf (accessed 11 September 2020).

Axford, N (2012) *Exploring Concepts of Child Well-being (Implications for Children's Services).* Policy Press.

Baranowsky, A B et al (2015) *Trauma Practice: Tools for Stabilization and Recovery (3rd ed).* Hogrefe Publishing.

Begikhani, N (2015) *Honour-based Violence (Experiences and Counter-strategies in Iraqi Kurdistan and the UL Kurdish Diaspora).* Ashgate Publishing.

Betts, A et al (2012) *UNHCR: The Politics and Practice of Refugee Protection (2nd ed).* Routledge.

Boyd, J et al (2018) Mindfulness-based Treatments for Post-traumatic Stress Disorder: A Review of the Treatment Literature and Neurobiological Evidence. *Journal of Psychiatry and Neuroscience*, 43(1): 7–25.

Brown, P and Calnan, M (2012) *Trusting on the Edge (Managing Uncertainty and Vulnerability in the Midst of Serious Mental Health Problems).* Policy Press.

Calais Writers (2017) *Voices from the 'Jungle': Stories from the Calais Refugee Camp.* Pluto Press.

Chase, E et al (2008) *The Emotional Well-being of Young People in the UK.* British Association for Adoption and Fostering (BAAF).

Cox, D and Pawar, M (2013) *International Social Work.* Sage Publications.

Crowther, S (2019) *Working with Asylum Seekers and Refugees.* Jessica Kingsley Publishers.

Curran, S et al (2013) *Working with Young People (2nd ed).* Sage Publications.

Davies, C and Ward, H (2013) *Safeguarding Children Across Services (Messages from Research).* Jessica Kingsley Publishers.

Department for Education (2014) *Care of Unaccompanied and Trafficked Children.* Department of Education.

Department for Education (2017) *Child Sexual Exploitation.* Department of Education.

Department of Health (1995) *Unaccompanied Asylum-seeking Children.* Department of Health.

Devenney, K (2019) Social Work with Unaccompanied Asylum-seeking Young People: Reframing Social Care Professionals as 'Co-navigators'. *The British Journal of Social Work*, 50(3): 926–43.

Dorling, K (2017) *Seeking Support – A Guide to the Rights and Entitlements of Separated Children.* Coram Children's Legal Centre.

Doyle, C (2012) *Working with Abused Children.* Palgrave Macmillan.

Egan, G (2014) *The Skilled Helper – A Client-centred Approach.* Cengage Learning.

Ellis, J and Thiara, R K (2014) *Preventing Violence Against Women and Girls (Educational Work with Children and Young People).* Policy Press.

European Migration Network (2018) *Approaches to Unaccompanied Minors Following Status Determination in the EU Plus Norway – Synthesis Report.* European Migration Network (EMN).

Evans, P and Kruger, A (2013) *Youth and Community Empowerment in Europe.* International Perspective.

Finn, M (2012) *Al-Qaeda and Sacrifice (Martyrdom, War and Politics).* Pluto Press.

Freedman, J (2015) *Gendering the International Asylum and Refugee Debate (2nd ed).* Palgrave Macmillan.

Goulden, C and D'Arcy, A (2014) A Definition of Poverty. JRF Programme Paper: Anti-poverty Strategies for the UK. York: Joseph Rowntree Foundation. [online] Available at: www.jrf.org.uk/report/definition-poverty (accessed 11 September 2020).

Gournay, K (2015) *Post-traumatic Stress Disorder: Recovery after Accident and Disaster.* Sheldon Press.

Gray, M and Webb, S A (2013) *The New Politics of Social Work.* Palgrave Macmillan.

Groark, C et al (2011) Understanding the Experiences and Emotional Needs of Unaccompanied Asylum-seeking Adolescents in the UK. *Clinical Child Psychology and Psychiatry*, 16(3): 421–42.

Hills, J (2015) *Good Times, Bad Times (The Welfare Myth of Them and Us).* Policy Press.

Home Office (2017) *An Inspection of How the Home Office Considers the 'Best Interests' of Unaccompanied Asylum Sekking Children.* Home Office.

Home Office (2019) *Assessing Age.* Home Office.

Hulewat, P (1996) Resettlement: A Cultural and Psychological Crisis. *Social Work*, 41(2): 129–35.

Jakobsen, M et al (2014) Prevalence of Psychiatric Disorders Among Unaccompanied Asylum-seeking Adolescents in Norway. *Clinical Practice and Epidemiology in Mental Health*, 10: 53–8.

Jeffery, B et al (2014) *Journeys in Community-based Research.* University of Regina Press.

Kelly, E and Bokhari, F (2012) *Safeguarding Children from Abroad (Refugee, Asylum Seeking and Trafficked Children in the UK).* Jessica Kingsley Publishers.

Kennerly, H (2009) *Overcoming Childhood Trauma: A Self-help Guide Using Cognitive Behavioural Techniques.* Constable and Robinson.

Kohli, R K S (2006) *Social Work with Unaccompanied Asylum-seeking Children.* Palgrave Macmillan.

Kohli, R K S (2007) *Working with Unaccompanied Asylum-seeking Children: Issues for Policy and Practice.* Palgrave Macmillan.

Kohli, R K S (2011) Working to Ensure Safety, Belonging and Success for Unaccompanied Asylum-seeking Children. *Child Abuse Review*, 20(5): 311–23.

Lewis, S J et al (2019) The Epidemiology of Trauma and Post-traumatic Stress Disorder in a Representative Cohort of Young People in England and Wales. *Lancet Psychiatry*, 6(3): 247–56.

Matthews, S et al (2014) *Approved Mental Health Practice (Essential Themes for Students and Practitioners).* Palgrave Macmillan.

Messina-Dysert, G (2015) *Rape Culture and Spiritual Violence (Religion, Testimony, and Visions of Healing).* Routledge.

Migrant Help (2017) *The Asylum Advice, Post Decision – Negative.* [online] Available at: www.migranthelpuk.org/Handlers/Download.ashx?IDMF=022acee2-fa23-4cef-a691-983050a7ada2 (accessed 17 July 2020).

Mollor, B (2015) *Refugees, Prisoners and Camps (A Functional Analysis of the Phenomenon of Encampment).* Palgrave Macmillan.

Nuttman-Shwartz, O and Levanon, O S (2019) Asylum Seekers in Israel: Challenges to Social Work. *The British Journal of Social Work*, 49(8): 2283–98.

Pearce, J et al (2013) *Trafficked Young People – Breaking the Wall of Silence.* Routledge.

Pilgrim, D (2014) *Key Concepts in Mental Health (3rd ed).* Sage Publications.

Rabasa, A and Bernard, C (2014) *Eurojihad (Pattern of Islamist Radicalisation and Terrorism in Europe).* Cambridge University Press.

Scharff Smith, P (2014) *When the Innocent are Punished (The Children of Imprisoned Parents).* Palgrave Macmillan.

Shaw, J and Frost, N (2013) *Young People and the Care Experience.* Routledge.

Shire, W (2011) *Teaching My Mother How to Give Birth.* Mouthmark Series.

Tait, A and Wosu, H (2013) *Direct Work with Vulnerable Children.* Jessica Kingsley Publishers.

Turbett, C (2014) *Doing Radical Social Work.* Palgrave Macmillan.

van Ee, E et al (2016) Parental PTSD, Adverse Parenting and Child Attachment in a Refugee Sample. *Attachment & Human Development*, 18(3): 273–91.

Wade, J et al (2012) *Fostering Unaccompanied Asylum-seeking Young People (Creating a Family Across a World of Difference).* British Association for Adoption and Fostering (BAAF).

Webber, F (2012) *Borderline Justice – The Fight for Refugee and Migrant Rights.* Pluto Press.

Wild, J (2013) *Exploiting Childhood.* Jessica Kingsley Publishers.

World Health Organization (2012) *The International Statistical Classification of Diseases and Health Related Problems, ICD-10 Hardcover.* World Health Organization.

# Index